CITIZEN'S PRIMER FOR
CONSERVATION ACTIVISM

How to Fight Development in Your Community

Judith Perlman

 University of Texas Press | **Austin**

First edition, 2004

Requests for permission to reproduce material from
this work should be sent to Permissions, University
of Texas Press, Box 7819, Austin, TX 78713-7819.

⊚ The paper used in this book meets the minimum
requirements of ANSI/NISO Z39.48-1992 (R1997)
(Permanence of Paper).

Library of Congress Cataloging-in-Publication Data
Perlman, Judith, 1952–
Citizen's primer for conservation activism : how to fight
development in your community / Judith Perlman.—
1st ed.
     p.   cm.
Includes index.

      ISBN 0-292-70290-6 (pbk. : alk. paper)

1. Environmentalism—Handbooks, manuals, etc.
I. Title.
GE195.P47   2004
333.72—dc22   2003027793

CITIZEN'S PRIMER FOR
CONSERVATION ACTIVISM

This book is dedicated to the
Friends of Fischer Creek.

Contents

Acknowledgments   ix

Introduction | 1

Chapter One: **Identify the Issues | 19**
(Knowledge Is Power)

Chapter Two: **Get Involved | 31**
(One Person Can Do a Lot)

Chapter Three: **Devise a Strategy | 45**
(Which Way Should We Go?)

Chapter Four: **Hire Counsel | 55**
("The First Thing We Do, Let's Kill All the Lawyers")

Chapter Five: **Build a Coalition and Partnerships | 69**
(Strange Bedfellows)

Chapter Six: **Influence Local Government | 86**
(Meetings, Meetings, Meetings)

Chapter Seven: **Conduct a Media Campaign | 103**
(Opening Pandora's Box)

Chapter Eight: **Fund-raising | 114**
(Money Makes the World Go 'Round)

Chapter Nine: **Opposing the Developer | 138**
(Bluster, Bully, and Bluff)

Chapter Ten: **Managing the Process | 152**
(Roller-coaster Ride)

Index   161

Acknowledgments

Writing a book is a lot harder than it looks. The process is a solitary experience, yet it took many people to help me through this lonely endeavor. I mention a few of you below, and my deepest thanks to everyone who helped me in ways large and small. John Kirsch loaned me his organized and complete files on the fight for Fischer Creek. I would have had great difficulty reconstructing those events if I had had to rely solely on my own filing system, which was to throw everything into a big box. Ann Grote-Pirrung, herself a writer, provided endless encouragement and the invaluable advice that I should "trust my voice." Vicki Johnson-Steger was a tireless reader, perpetual cheerleader, and sister in spirit. Bob and Erica Heuel, both accomplished artists, provided empathy, as I struggled with the creative process, along with bottomless cups of coffee at dawn. Their unflagging conviction in the cause and in my work got me started on many difficult days. My brother, Dr. Baron Perlman, himself a published scholar, held my hand throughout the process, from inception to index. He's the perfect combination of experienced mentor and big brother. My friend Phyllis Doersch kept me on the path from day to day with walking, yoga, and her supreme confidence that this would be the first book of many. My faithful and furry friend Vronsky kept me company through long hours at the computer. He was delighted with my commitment because I was home all the time and needed to break up the tedium with lots of walks. Finally, thanks to friend and chef extraordinaire Steve Matson who fed me and took care of me while I wrote this book.

CITIZEN'S PRIMER FOR
CONSERVATION ACTIVISM

Introduction

This book is written for you . . .

If you are frustrated at seeing unwanted development threaten your community.

If you are sick of seeing your taxes increase to pay for all the services needed by so much "progress."

If the high point of your day is seeing a great blue heron wade in a stream or a red fox cross the road.

If you cherish a scenic view of a lake or meadow on your morning walk or evening commute.

If you want to preserve a woodlot, creek, or wetland for your children to explore.

If you value darkness so that you can see the night sky.

If you mourn the loss of quiet and solitude.

If you are frustrated at urban sprawl and the traffic, noise, and pollution it brings.

If you are angry that out-of-town landowners control the future of your neighborhood.

If you are "mad as hell" and don't want to take it anymore.

This book is written for you, if you want to do something about it but do not know what to do or where to start.

You *can* do something. More and more, individuals are fighting to protect the communities they inhabit and love. To an ordinary citizen trying to stop the steamroller of development, the force of big money allied with government may seem unstoppable. But just as David slew Goliath, individuals and small groups of citizens are challenging these forces and winning. Each time this happens, I think of it as a miracle—a miracle of hard work, a miracle of democracy, a miracle of free press, sometimes just a miracle.

These victories are all the more miraculous because there is little support for citizens who want to take on The System by fighting development and the reaches of government that support development. For each of these skirmishes, citizens are making it up as they go along. Primarily local in nature, land battles are fought in isolation, without the experience or support of others who have done it before. There's no how-to manual on what to do and what to expect, on what works and what does not work. Every land battle has unique elements—distinctive personalities, different laws and regulations, local politics, and its own historical context. Yet there are also common themes and lessons to these David-against-Goliath battles that are occurring in communities throughout the country.

This book is for ordinary citizens who want to *do* something. It is my intention to provide a handbook of practical information on how to fight unwanted development in your community. It is intended to give you an outline of what to do and what to expect if you get involved in a development fight. Often, there is tremendous time pressure and the need to learn fast and act fast. I wrote this book intending that people might read and absorb it quickly. The book is for strategizing around the kitchen table, not ponderous research. It is meant to provide a lot of ideas but cannot possibly cover every issue in every situation. Rather, it is a starting point to get you in and get you going. You will have to research the facts and devise the strategy that's right for your unique situation. But this book does provide a framework for addressing your situation and determining whether you can buck The System. In many circumstances, you can. You can make a miracle happen in your backyard.

Everybody has a story, and this is mine. The observations and examples in this book are based on my own experience in three different land battles, all of which occurred in Wisconsin. The themes of each land battle, however, are familiar everywhere. In order for you to get the most from the examples in the book, it will help to know my background. Throughout the book, I refer to these three land battles as "Fischer Creek," "Point Creek," and "Hika Conservancy." I hope that you will be able to identify with facets of my story.

I moved to the Village of Cleveland, Wisconsin, for its quiet rural beauty, undeveloped Lake Michigan shoreline, and low-stress lifestyle. I came to this village, located 66 miles north of Milwaukee, by way of a stressful career in Chicago. First a lawyer, then a business executive for the derivatives trading unit of an international bank, I found my life was a pressure cooker. I faced long hours, international travel, and the intense stress of working for options traders who made million-dollar decisions in a matter of seconds. On the personal front, my health was not strong. I never fully recovered from a serious car accident several years earlier, and my recurrent health problems caused me to be hospitalized regularly. While I was in the hospital, I worked; after my discharge, I continued to work. Work defined my life.

Now, my former life sounds ghastly. But at the time, walking away from my career and familiar life in Chicago was the hardest decision I had ever made. I purchased my cottage in Cleveland in the spring of 1994 as a weekend house to escape the rat race. I soon concluded that this little village of approximately thirteen hundred people was an undiscovered jewel. Mainly a bedroom community for the neighboring small cities of Manitowoc to the north and Sheboygan to the south, Cleveland had quiet historic neighborhoods, creeks and woodlots, weekend cottages on breathtaking Lake Michigan views, and surrounding homestead dairy farms.

By the end of August 1994, I had decided to make Cleveland my permanent home. I had found a time and place to heal and rest. I gave my employer two weeks' notice after Labor Day, put my condo on the market, and arrived the third week in September, ready to plant my garden, watch the birds, and take long walks on country roads and sandy beaches. My biggest project was finding a puppy.

The story of Fischer Creek

The week I arrived to begin my new "permanent" life in Cleveland, I saw a public notice posted at the Cleveland post office for a Cleveland Plan Commission meeting to discuss "Hika Cove." I had heard rumors that someone was proposing a condominium development along Lake Michigan just north of Cleveland in the Town of Centerville, in an area locally referred to as "Fischer Creek." I wondered if "Hika Cove" referred to that condominium project.

I had never been to a plan commission meeting—or any local government meeting, for that matter. On a whim, I decided to attend along with a friend who had a weekend home on the beach. There were about a dozen other people in the audience. We did not know another soul. The purpose of the meeting was to discuss a planned unit development to be located at Fischer Creek.

Fischer Creek encompassed approximately 130 acres of undeveloped land, including wetland, bluff, meadow, and woodland—habitat for numerous plant and animal species. The creek itself is classified as a Class I trout stream by the Wisconsin Department of Natural Resources, a designation recognizing high water quality and habitat for spawning lake trout and salmon. The entire parcel contains a meandering creek, prominent dunes that elongate in a direction perpendicular to Lake Michigan, and almost a mile of undeveloped Lake Michigan beach. The area is home to four major wetland communities—sedge meadow, bluff seeps, shrub swamp, and wood swamp. There are three major upland communities—old-field community, successional forest, and mature upland forest. Although privately owned by an out-of-state landowner for years, Fischer Creek had been used and appreciated by area residents for its excellent fishing, sandy beaches, varied habitat, and remote location.

At the plan commission meeting were the chairman and members of the plan commission; the village president, Gary Schmitz; and a developer from Chicago, Gerald Fogelson. It was obvious to me that Fogelson was a city slicker, in spite of the fact that he had "dressed down" for the occasion. In a deliberately casual crewneck sweater, khaki pants, and leather tassled loafers, he had shed his suit and tie to become a local "good old boy" for the evening.

Fogelson had a simple layout for a proposed planned unit development for the Fischer Creek area, which subdivided the bluff and lake frontage into a long, narrow row of lots lined up side by side like soldiers in formation. The terrain of the landscape was completely unconsidered in the preliminary site plan. It was apparent that he had invested almost nothing in his design plans. He proposed a 150-unit gated community, primarily second homes and condominiums for affluent Chicago and Milwaukee residents. According to Fogelson, lots would be priced from $150,000 to $450,000, and there would be strict architectural standards for houses built. Schmitz nodded his head approvingly.

The developer's timetable called for the village to make fast approvals and for construction to begin in a few months. He wanted to break ground that winter. He left the impression that the houses would sell like hotcakes, the development would assuredly be a big success, and Cleveland would benefit immeasurably from the addition of Hika Cove. In short, Fogelson was coming to town and throwing money at us. All we had to do was catch it.

Fischer Creek is located in the Town of Centerville. The Village of Cleveland was involved because Fogelson needed annexation of the land from Centerville to the village. Without Cleveland's sewer and water services, the proposed development would have to use septic, mound, or holding tanks for sanitary services, and wells for water. This was not optimal for upper-income housing. Also, Centerville's zoning regulations mandated lower density than Cleveland's planned unit development zoning category. It is generally the case that developers want to build as many units as they can in a given location, and Fogelson was no exception. At the meeting, Fogelson, Schmitz, and others talked as though approval of the development were a "done deal."

I was appalled at the proposal, as well as at the seemingly cavalier way that the village was about to approve this decision. The other residents at the meeting were similarly upset, and we agreed to meet again later that week. The following Saturday, we gathered at the local diner, where about a dozen neighbors expressed concern, anger, and frustration. Some people opposed the development for environmental reasons; others were concerned about what this would do to the character of the community. Still others wanted more information before making up their minds. Everyone was upset by the village's intention to "railroad" an approval on a short timetable without public input. At the time, I did not label myself an environmentalist, but I could see that such a development would have a huge effect on the village in many ways. This one development would increase by 50 percent the number of residences in Cleveland. I wanted to slow down the process and get some answers. I believed that the citizens should be heard on the issue. It was incredible to me that a few village "fathers" could ram a change of this magnitude through without holding public hearings and considering the will of the community.

Thus began the Friends of Fischer Creek and our yearlong odyssey to fight "Hika Cove" and preserve Fischer Creek in its natural state. The initial concerns of a few citizens became a bitter community battle.

On the political front, the developer needed to annex the land from Centerville to Cleveland, which required a two-thirds affirmative vote of the Village of Cleveland Board of Trustees. Residents of Cleveland were divided on the issue of annexation. Those in favor of the development believed it would help the tax base and help pay for a newly mandated wastewater treatment plant, as well as represent "progress" for the village. Centerville did not want to lose a big piece of land (and tax base) to Cleveland, and had important interests in the conflict as well. For the most part, the Friends of Fischer Creek were allied with many residents of Centerville to defeat the annexation. However, like the village, the town was also divided. Whereas many town residents did not want to cede a big piece of land to the village, or, for environmental reasons, did not want to see Fischer Creek developed, there were those who, for the added tax base, wanted the development to occur in the town rather than in the village.

In addition to local politics, money soon became an important issue. Even if we defeated the annexation at this time, the issue would return again and again as development pressures pushed up the lakefront. In defeating one petition for annexation, we were not assured of continued success as petition after petition was filed seeking to annex and develop for profit this highly desirable parcel. The law of odds made it almost inevitable that a developer would appear with enough money and power to succeed. Therefore, the only way to preserve Fischer Creek permanently was to buy it. Now the Friends of Fischer Creek were faced with the struggle to amass the $1.3 million needed to purchase it. Back in 1994, that amount of money could best be raised in a short time frame from the government. Consequently we became embroiled in state and county financial and political matters as well.

When I moved to Cleveland, I had no idea I would spend the next twelve months on a conservation battle against local politicians and Chicago developers. It was not the relaxing, bucolic life I had signed up for. But I viewed defense of those values as an investment that would benefit me for the rest of my life.

Due to the strenuous efforts of a lot of people—and some incredible luck—we defeated the annexation, at the same time raising $1.3 million for the State of Wisconsin to purchase Fischer Creek for a new State Conservation Area. The Wisconsin Department of Natural Resources, in a check signed by then governor Tommy Thompson, awarded a one-million-dollar stewardship fund grant toward the purchase. Manitowoc County (through some clever internal political maneuvering by our supporters) approved $300,000 to complete the transaction. Fischer Creek became a model in the State of Wisconsin for a state–local conservation partnership in which Manitowoc County, pursuant to a written management agreement, manages land in conservation owned by the state.

Today, you can travel to southeastern Manitowoc County and visit the Fischer Creek Conservation Area. You can fish for trout off the 150-year-old iron bridge spanning the creek near its mouth at Lake Michigan. You can walk pristine sandy beaches and cool off on a sweltering summer day. You can set up a scope and watch the migrating red-throated loons in early spring. You can walk a trail through dense woods and listen to the wind and waves. Fischer Creek is preserved forever for all people to enjoy. I talk to visitors at Fischer Creek and tell them the story of the fight for Fischer Creek. I let them know that they are walking on a miracle.

The story of Point Creek

In the years following Fischer Creek, I was not involved in any major conservation issues. I served on the village board for a few months to fill a vacancy, but the service did not suit me. I struggled with more health problems. I became a member of the Village of Cleveland and Town of Centerville Joint Plan Commission, on which Cleveland and Centerville worked together to create a joint land-use plan. This cooperation between neighboring municipalities on a land-use plan was groundbreaking in Wisconsin. The work was alternately exciting and tedious, but we did succeed in creating a joint plan and joint land-use district maps that both town and village enacted. Tensions sometimes run high between town and village, but we are proud to have created land-use districts that were defined at least in part by the actual land configuration and historic use, not by municipal boundaries.

In 1999 my friend Rolf Johnson lured me onto the board of the local land conservancy. Rolf had been one of the key leaders of the Friends of Fischer Creek. Back then Rolf articulated a vision to preserve an extended watershed of approximately fifteen hundred acres, north and west of Fischer Creek, through a combination of public land and private conservation easement. He wanted to create a biological island out of the Great Lakes Watershed, which in his opinion was of tremendous scientific and social importance, given the necessity of clean, fresh water for the world. During the fight for Fischer Creek, Rolf promoted this vision, but most of us put our immediate attention on what needed to be done to preserve Fischer Creek. When we were done, we were all exhausted and had no energy left for tackling a new project. We needed to rest, and the community needed to heal.

After several years' respite, I thought it might be time to think about Rolf's vision. I was willing to "stick my toe in the water"—that's it!—in terms of commitment to another conservation project.

Inspired by what we did at Fischer Creek, several citizens in Sheboygan (ten miles south of Cleveland) formed the Sheboygan Area Land Conservancy. Their mission was to preserve open space in the counties of Sheboygan, Manitowoc (where Fischer Creek is), and Fond du Lac, primarily through the tool of conservation easement, which is a voluntary arrangement between a landowner and a land conservancy providing for permanent conservation of land.

At Rolf's request, and after meeting with me, the land conservancy board welcomed me as a new member. I do not like meetings and was not looking for a big commitment. The land conservancy board was a pleasant, low-key group, and I thought I could handle one meeting a month in that setting. After my contentious and exhausting experience with Fischer Creek, I found the land conservancy appealing because conservation easements involve collaborating one-on-

one with landowners who have a conservation ethic and are preserving their land voluntarily and happily. No more battles! I was looking to work with a few Manitowoc County landowners in the nearby Lake Michigan Watershed.

A few months after I joined the land conservancy board, we learned that an out-of-state landowner filed a variance request with Manitowoc County for an extended cul-de-sac at Point Creek. The landowner needed the road to facilitate a seventeen-lot subdivision of upscale homes. Point Creek is about two miles north of Fischer Creek, and the other "jewel in the crown" of Rolf's vision for a biological island along the shores of Lake Michigan.

The Point Creek parcel is thirty-nine acres, with twenty-seven hundred feet of pristine Lake Michigan beach and contains the tallest sand dunes in Manitowoc County, as well as estuary, bluff, coastal canyon, beach, meadow, and pinewoods. Numerous scientific studies had attested to the habitat and unusual geological and biological features of the site, and had identified it as an important stopping point for migratory birds on the Lake Michigan flyway. Point Creek is also home to a large congregation (more than a hundred individuals) of great blue herons that use the site as their primary habitat during the spring and summer months after they fledgling their young.

Moreover, Point Creek adjoins two other pieces of land already in conservation; if we were able to save the Point Creek parcel, the total land in conservation would be 138 contiguous acres, including 4,400 feet of Lake Michigan shoreline and 1,000 feet of creek bank.

Initially, Rolf was spearheading the effort to save Point Creek. Despite the obvious conservation values of the site, I was a reluctant participant. Out of loyalty to Rolf and some commitment to the cause, I participated, but in a far more limited way than for Fischer Creek, which I had thrown myself into heart and soul.

For many reasons, I just did not feel committed to the parcel in the same way as for Fischer Creek. A lot of the fight for Fischer Creek had to do with enabling democracy and ensuring community participation in decisions affecting our future. I became conservation-minded during my work on Fischer Creek, but my reasons for participation were never just about conservation. Also, Point Creek was geographically farther from me, and the struggle appeared to be mainly about raising money, a task I did not relish. By early 2000 I had just started a business, and my time and energy were committed to that venture. Finally, I did not see much chance of success in saving Point Creek. The landowner wanted an exorbitant price for the land—$1.9 million. Times had changed, and the era of 100 percent financing from the state was over. It would be much tougher to raise the money, and a significant portion would have to come from the private sector. I did not see it happening in a community of old-line manufacturing firms and small dairy farms.

Rolf, however, is a perennial optimist and an ace fund-raiser. Rolf and I, along with Mike Sorenson, the cochairman of the land conservancy, made a presentation at the West Foundation, a philanthropic organization serving Manitowoc County. The West Foundation had never funded a land-conservation project before, but we gave it our best shot. To my surprise, we received a $250,000 two-for-one matching grant. We would receive $250,000 from the West Foundation if we raised another $500,000 in donations and pledges. That was great, but where in the world would we come up with another $500,000?

Largely through Rolf's efforts and connections and because of an anonymous $200,000 donation we received, we met the terms of the grant, to my amazement. A war chest of $750,000—even though mostly pledges—is impressive fund-raising in Manitowoc County. But we still had $1.25 million to go. Rolf requested a grant from the Wisconsin Department of Natural Resources (DNR) Stewardship Program, which could potentially provide up to 50 percent of the DNR-appraised value of the land. We commissioned two appraisals for the DNR grant. Both came in significantly lower than the landowner's $1.9 million demand. Even if we got a grant from the DNR, we were still going to be short by $600,000.

Then Rolf received a cancer diagnosis. He went from fighting for Point Creek to fighting for his life. As I looked at the other members of the land conservancy board, it was obvious that no one could take up leadership on Point Creek. Rolf was so committed to Point Creek that I thought the outcome might be a matter of life and death for him. I did not want him to worry about Point Creek while he was battling cancer, so I agreed to take it on and see what I could do.

The task was overwhelming, and I proposed a consulting arrangement with the land conservancy board so that I could be paid something for my efforts. I simply could not afford to abandon my new business for months with no alternate source of income. The task at hand required a sophisticated skill set using my experience in law and business and would be tremendously time-consuming. It was not inappropriate, I concluded, for the organization to pay something for the time and talent that was needed to run the project. The land conservancy had no paid employees, so this was a first step for them in terms of working with a professional staff person.

The Department of Natural Resources came through with an initial allocation of $600,000, subject to further approvals. I managed to identify, write, and win additional grants giving us sufficient funds to meet the owner's $1.9 million price. During the state's 2002 budget crisis, we waged a major lobbying effort in Madison to keep the stewardship grant that we had been awarded.

Meanwhile, we had problems on the other side of the transaction, in terms of negotiating a purchase agreement for the property. The landowner, a Colorado family partnership represented by Stan Lee, refused to budge on the asking price and was actively shopping the parcel to other purchasers, as well as regularly threatening to "bring in the bulldozers." Stan also had a tendency to terminate negotiations regularly and required an enormous amount of "hand-holding." He doubted we were a viable purchaser because we had not come up with the money in over a year, yet we also seemed to be his best chance of getting his $1.9 million.

Peter Mayer, the lawyer who represented the Friends of Fischer Creek, agreed to negotiate with and handle Stan. Peter had the daunting task of alleviating Stan Lee's considerable anxiety, building credibility for the land conservancy as a viable purchaser—even as we scrambled for funds—and reaching a legal agreement that would satisfy Stan, protect the land conservancy and pass muster with two different government agencies that award grants.

We had a lot of ups and downs finalizing the purchase. But on June 19, 2002, the governor of Wisconsin, Scott McCallum, came to Cleveland to dedicate the Point Creek Natural Area, purchased with $1.4 million in state and federal money, and $500,000 in private donations. If you visit southeastern Manitowoc County, in Wisconsin, you can visit the Point Creek Natural Area and see scientists from three partnering universities conducting field research, watch more than a hundred great blue herons fledgling their young, and sight an occasional bald eagle. How did we pull it off? A lot of hard work by a few people, and some more luck. Another miracle.

The ongoing story of Hika Conservancy

As I was working furiously on Point Creek, developers bought a parcel of land near and dear to my heart. The Hika (pronounced High-Kah) Conservancy parcel is only 150 feet from my property. It borders the property of my next-door neighbor and extends to Centerville Creek and Hika Park on the other side. The initial proposal was for thirty-six condominiums. Of all the projects I had worked on, this was the first that was truly in my backyard!

The four-acre Hika Conservancy land included 535 feet of sandy Lake Michigan beach, a ridge and swale dune formation, wetland, a wooded area, and a meadow. The beach is accessible without traversing a bluff, which is unusual on this side of Lake Michigan. Despite its small acreage, Hika Conservancy is host to numerous migratory birds and animals and is part of the Centerville Creek Watershed. Several state and scientific studies have identified important aspects of the land.

Hika Park is Cleveland's only park on Lake Michigan and is known mainly for its boat ramp, used by area fishermen. A small beach adjoins the boat ramp, but the area is too small to accommodate both swimmers and boaters safely. As the population grows, Hika Park will be wholly inadequate in a few years. I envision people crammed into little Hika Park, while a vast expanse of beach remains unused by all except a handful of beachfront landowners. Many residents of the Hika neighborhood around the park have an alternate vision in which the undeveloped land is added to Hika Park. In that scenario, present residents and future generations will have public access to the beach and to a natural area for observation of wildlife and passive recreation.

Initially, the developers who purchased Hika Conservancy floated a proposal for a thirty-six-unit condominium development. After the community protested and village officials took a close look at the ordinances, the developers abandoned that proposal. They returned with a vague proposal for lower-density "townhouse condominiums" and filed a formal petition to change the zoning. The developers never offered a site plan and never proposed a specific number of units. They wanted to develop, in their own words, "as many as the site will allow."

Hika Park is located in Cleveland's historic Hika neighborhood. Featuring nineteenth-century cream brick homes, a few old businesses, and lakefront cottages, the neighborhood includes an active local history group, which studies and cherishes the history of Hika and even contemplated getting the neighborhood designated a historic preservation area. It is a close community of single-family residences in which children fish off the bridge and play in the streets and people don't lock their doors. The Hika neighborhood was clearly opposed to the incursion of condominiums owned by non-permanent residents, but members of the village board valued the potential tax base more than preservation of the neighborhood.

Although my heart was in Hika, my time was largely committed to Point Creek. My next-door neighbors, Otto and Laurel Wimpffen, agreed to take the lead. As neighbors to the site, they had the biggest interest and the most to lose, as well as certain legal rights afforded to contiguous landowners affected by a petition for rezoning. Otto and Laurel live in Chicago and use their cottage in Cleveland on weekends. However, they intend to retire here in a few years and are interested in issues affecting the community that would someday be their permanent home.

As a full-time resident and a neighbor, I served as a liaison between the Wimpffens and the community. I attended meetings in Cleveland, talked to village board members and employees, and helped organize community support against the zoning change, while at the same time keeping abreast of the Wimpffens' legal research and strategy.

The fight for the Hika Conservancy is continuing. The battle occurred first on the legal front, with Otto and Laurel hiring Peter Mayer to represent their interests. It was an expensive proposition for the couple, because counsel is not cheap. However, I am convinced that it was mainly their commitment that deterred the developers from pursuing either condominiums or townhouses on the site. We reduced our "worst-case scenario" from thirty-six condominium units to five or six single-family homes. In terms of consistency with the historic Hika neighborhood, the community could live with the latter.

However, many of us wanted to see the lakeshore in public rather than private hands. Therefore, we encouraged the village to buy the conservancy as an extension of Hika Park. It is interesting that, in many communities, lake property owners band together to keep the public off "their" beaches. In Cleveland, almost all the lakeshore owners are encouraging public access to the beach. Nonetheless, convincing village board members to forgo short-term tax revenues for the long-term benefits of maintaining public access to the lakefront was an uphill battle.

Through both expensive lawyering and grassroots politicking, we made tremendous progress on the issue. When the developers first proposed condominiums, the board rejected a proposal to purchase the Hika Conservancy and went so far as to pass a resolution stating that they would never discuss the issue again. Less than a year later, the board voted to explore purchasing the land; six months later they had entered into an agreement with the developers to purchase the land as a park and applied for several government grants.

The problem then turned from political to economic—finding the money. Because of the legal barriers to a zoning change (which would permit higher density on the parcel), the developers are willing sellers—for now. I doubt that they have suddenly become "tree huggers." Rather, they probably see purchase by the village of the entire parcel as the fastest way for them to recoup their money and move on. Whether the village can raise the money, about $530,000, and stay committed to the purchase remains to be seen. If the purchase fails, we return to a political fight on zoning and appropriate use for the neighborhood.

Land battles share common issues.

While each of my land battles—and yours—involves different facts, there are many common issues and problems.

You are dealing with multiple personalities and parties, including the landowner; the developer (who may or may not be the same person as the landowner); and various boards, committees, agencies, and commissions of local, state, and even federal government.

You are dealing with complex issues involving land-use ordinances, zoning changes, site plan development, annexation and civil procedure, and business and economic issues concerning developer financing, tax base, and cost of services.

You will be engaged in fund-raising, from soliciting small amounts to fund your operating expenses, to larger amounts to cover legal fees and other professional services, up to multimillion-dollar sums to fund land acquisition. You may be writing grants and working through complicated requirements for federal, state, or endowment funding.

You will come up against vested interests in government and business. You may have to speak out at public meetings or fight for the attention of public officials.

You will be dealing with lawyers, both your own and those on the other side.

You will have to build a coalition and find partners.

You will be dealing with the press, including newspaper reporters and editors.

What is in this book?

This book offers practical insight and examples for dealing with the many issues common to land battles in different communities.

Chapter One discusses the information you will need to embark on a land battle. It will help you determine whether or not you have any basis to challenge development and where to go from there. It sets forth a lot of specific issues for you to think about and research, from tax consequences and the economic effects of development, to habitat preservation and the economic value of open space. This chapter suggests where to get that information, such as from local government, state government, universities, not-for-profit conservation organizations, lawyers, developers, and planners. It also sets forth some of the legal issues you may need to understand, such as required government procedures relating to open meetings, postings, time periods, and public hearings; rights of neighbors for zon-

ing changes; state and local issues relating to annexation; preliminary plat requirements; setback and shoreline ordinances; and other
environmental regulations. Finally, it encourages you to ask a lot of
questions and to question all the information you do gather.

Chapter Two is for people who are not sure they can accomplish
anything on their own. It provides information and examples of just
how much one person or a small group can do. In a democracy, individuals are afforded many rights, such as gathering information, attending public meetings, speaking publicly, lobbying, writing letters,
petitioning, distributing leaflets, hiring a lawyer, raising money, and
contacting the media. This chapter encourages a good hard look at
what motivates you and gives a realistic appraisal of the time and
energy required in such an undertaking. It also discusses some of
the other resources you may need and gives examples of the kinds
of information an individual can get and how that information can
be used in your land battle. It discusses how a leadership circle will
naturally form, so that you will not be working alone for long, and
concludes with some examples of how just a few people achieved
major victories in fighting development.

Chapter Three deals with the critical task of devising a strategy,
giving examples from other land battles. It posits the importance of
strategy in providing focus for your time and effort, which can otherwise be dissipated on nonproductive matters. It also suggests action
steps for implementing your chosen strategy.

Chapter Four discusses the role of lawyers in a land battle. It discusses why it is likely that you will need a lawyer at some point in
an extended land battle. It sets forth some of the ways a lawyer can
help you, such as by keeping local government honest, by advocating interpretations of the law favorable to your position, by helping
implement your strategy, by acting as a lightening rod for conflict, by
negotiating a land contract, and by dealing with other lawyers. This
chapter also discusses how to find and retain counsel and how to
manage the fees. It provides examples of the strategic use of counsel
in different land battle scenarios.

Chapter Five discusses the importance of building a grassroots
coalition and partnerships and explains how to go about it. It discusses the importance of building community support, even if you

initially think you do not need it. This chapter describes how to build a coalition, from choosing a name to distributing written materials. It advises you on how to use your supporters most effectively and to be open to "strange bedfellows." It encourages you to hold your own meetings and suggests other ways to build support. Finally, the chapter discusses the importance of forming partnerships with other organizations. It provides examples of why such partnerships are important, and gives ideas about what kinds of organizations to approach and what to ask for.

Chapter Six gets into the difficult task of influencing local government. It sets forth two scenarios, that of a local government that is basically supportive of your goals, and that of a local government that supports development and is unreceptive to conservation proposals. This chapter provides specific suggestions on how to deal with the government as a friend as well as an adversary and gives examples of tactics that did or did not work in different land battles. It discusses the sensitivities of local government and specific actions for confronting those sensitivities in a way that will bring you success. Finally, the chapter posits the eventuality of voting out of office certain intransigent government officials, and the importance of public service as part of your long-term plan.

Chapter Seven discusses the role of the media in a land battle. It puts forth some of the problems with publicity, as well as the benefits, to help you determine whether or not you want publicity. It lists different types of media coverage, with examples of how each was used in previous land battles. This chapter also describes some of the different personalities and skill sets that may be necessary for a media campaign. Finally, it recounts the media campaign for Fischer Creek and gives examples of editorials and how they fit into an ongoing land battle.

Chapter Eight takes on the issue of fund-raising. It discusses why you will need money, from incidental expenses for postage and printing, to the more significant costs of professional counsel, all the way to raising millions of dollars for land acquisition. It tells you how to organize for fund-raising and provides ideas on how to raise money for operational expenses. This chapter also discusses the very different task of fund-raising the sizable amount necessary to purchase a piece of land. It describes the kinds of organizational structure and partners you will need and details several fund-raising campaigns. It gives specific pointers, from developing the right relationships to tips on writing and documenting the grant application itself. Using the example of Point Creek, Chapter Eight recounts the process of getting a public grant, from application through all the intermediary stages on the way to receiving a check. Finally, it compares grants from public sources and from private foundations, and discusses raising money from wealthy individuals.

Chapter Nine delves into the dynamic of dealing with a landowner or developer. It describes how developers make money, so that you can understand their motivation and also their weak points. The chapter sets forth general principles for dealing with developers, as well as how to recognize and counter typical developer tactics such as blustering, bullying, bluffing, threatening, and attempting to divide and conquer the community. It provides numerous questions for you to ask concerning a proposed development and provides sample responses to typical developer propositions.

Finally, Chapter Ten tries to help you manage your expectations and tells you how to deal with the inherent stress of undertaking a land battle. Using both Fischer Creek and Point Creek as examples, this chapter describes the many ups and downs of a land battle and offers suggestions for managing the stresses specific to a battle against development.

I hope you decide to fight for control of your community, so that *you* decide the character of the place in which you live. I also hope this book helps you make that decision and helps you succeed in your fight. You will have more ups and downs in a short time than you ever thought possible. You may find yourself doing things you never thought you would be able to do. You may find friends and allies among people you never knew. Whether you win or lose, you will be glad you tried. Some of you will be rewarded with a miracle.

CHAPTER ONE

IDENTIFY THE ISSUES
(Knowledge Is Power)

Why bother?

One of the operating principles of my life is that knowledge is power. You should acquire as much information as possible related to your own unique conservation battle. You may not know exactly where and how it will help you, but I guarantee it *will* help you in countless ways:

- It will help you formulate a strategy.
- It will give you power and credibility to counteract inaccurate statements about the law, public policy, procedure, taxation, and economics.
- It will help you understand the motivations underlying the actions and positions of the other players.
- It will help you reframe the developer's issues and local government's issues in your own agenda.
- It will help you understand and predict behavior.
- It will give you authority to communicate with your community and with the press.

For all these reasons, take the time and effort to understand the underlying issues.

First decision: Can I do anything?

The most important priority at the first stage is to determine whether or not you can deter or influence the proposed development. Some situations are nonstarters. If land is going to be developed consistent with the current zoning, you may not be able to prevent the development from occurring. That determination depends on the particular requirements of your local zoning and development laws. Typically, you can exert influence when a change is requested or an approval needs to be granted. You need to intercede when a governing body has a choice as to whether a development should proceed, and convince that body to say no. The request may be for a change in zoning, approval of a site plan, variance, conditional use, or annexation, for example. Never underestimate the power of a lot of vocal, unhappy people at a meeting.

For example, if land is zoned for single-family houses and someone wants to put in a single-family house, there may not be anything you can do to stop the development. You might like the meadow behind your house, but as a practical matter, there may not be any mechanism for preventing construction.

Even if a zoning change is not needed, however, you may have other circumstances in which to influence events. It would be interesting to know how long the zoning has been in effect, whether zoning was changed legally with all required notices and hearings, and what the site plan requirements are. Perhaps wetlands or environmental setbacks prevent building on the site. With larger developments, you may be able to influence the site planning process in terms of design, drainage, erosion control, density, landscaping, lighting, and numerous other features.

In short, you need to understand the issues in order to understand your opportunities to affect the process. Ask the following questions:

- How is the land currently zoned?
- Does the current zoning permit the proposed use?
- Is the zoning consistent with any land-use plans in effect?
- Is the proposal consistent with the zoning and site plan requirements?
- Should a variance or conditional use be required?
- Would a zoning change be needed?
- What procedural requirements have to be followed?
- Do certain neighbors have statutory rights of notice or protest with

regard to the proposal? (Sometimes contiguous property owners or property owners within a certain distance have legal rights to notice or have the right to file a formal protest to a zoning change.)
• Are you sure? (Do not take at face value the first answer to any of these questions, especially if that answer comes from local government or someone with an interest in the outcome.)

Questions on any of the above topics provide opportunities for citizen input into the process. Often, the answers are not absolutely clear. Does a proposal require a zoning change, a variance, or a conditional use? It may require some research for you to know what position to take, depending on what is permitted and what your rights are. Educate yourself on the land-use categories and the approval process so that you can advocate your position.

Here's an example of why it is important to ask, "Are you sure?" One land-use dispute involved a trailer park that wanted to expand into an undeveloped woodlot. Village of Cleveland officials and the developer worked from a zoning map provided by the village, which showed the woodlot as properly zoned for the expansion. One concerned citizen went to the county courthouse, looked up the official land designations, and learned that the developer wanted to expand into a conservancy area, which was strictly prohibited. Case closed. Without one citizen's research and intervention, the village may have permitted numerous trees to be felled for an expanding trailer park.

Know the enemy.

Another way of looking at the gathering of information is: Know the Enemy. While the process of understanding the issues may be tedious, think of it as serious counterintelligence work. The more you know about the force you are opposing—be it developer, landowner, or government—the better you can ascertain their weaknesses and vulnerabilities. This knowledge will be invaluable as you devise a strategy and carry out your action plan. It will help you calculate the probability of success of various strategies and actions. It will help you understand the actions and countermoves of others as they occur.

The issues may change: Be forewarned.

Sometimes, as land disputes progress, the issues identified at the start don't change. For Point Creek, the developer demanded $1.9 million at the start. For two and a half years, we tried to raise $1.9 million. Point Creek appeared to be about money and it was about money. Nonetheless, some issues dropped out and some appeared along the way. Initially, when we thought we might be able to negotiate on price with the landowner, a key issue was valuation. We learned about the development rules for lakeshore construction, such as minimum setbacks and view lines, and the likelihood of owners receiving variances as to lot size or setback, and we educated ourselves about the market for property fronting Lake Michigan. As the landowner remained intransigent in his willingness to negotiate, the key issue became raising money to meet his price.

If we had not been successful in raising $1.9 million, we had a backup plan that involved challenging any proposed development on a number of grounds. We identified various issues that we might use to challenge development, including questioning the legality of the variance issued for the cul-de-sac, monitoring setbacks for home sites, and exploring state requirements for sewage and wastewater disposal. Luckily, we did not need our backup plan for Point Creek and so never researched those issues in depth.

In the fight for Fischer Creek, developer and village initially maintained that there were no issues that needed public discussion—only a few technical approvals were needed. Upon being questioned by citizens, village officials stated that their rationale for the development was to add to the tax base—growth being positive in and of itself—and to facilitate "progress," meaning add this upscale housing development, in the village of Cleveland. With a little digging, citizens identified many other issues related to the decision of annexation and approval of the development, such as the effect on residents' sewer and water rates, traffic, tax base, community, and the environment. Several issues lurked beneath the surface, such as years of accumulated dissatisfaction with village officials over previous and unrelated political issues, and even whether certain village officials may have gained personally or been promised a financial reward from the development.

As part of my self-education on development, I talked to lawyers in Chicago who represent developers. In these frank, off-the-record discussions, they told me how a big Chicago developer does business in a small town. Direct and indirect remuneration of key local officials is part of their bag of tricks, in the form of bribes or promises of jobs in the future development. We never publicly mentioned this last issue—whether anyone was "on the take"—in the fight for Fischer Creek. Nor have I ever seen evidence that any village official was set to benefit personally from the development.

But the issue was on my mind and affected our strategy and actions. It was not anything we knew for certain; it was not anything we raised publicly; and it was not anything we ever looked to prove, but it was always in the back of my mind. The information helped predict and explain behavior that might otherwise have seemed irrational. It helped focus our attention on people who might be convinced by us on the issues and not waste time on people who might be motivated by something that we could not counter with reason and public support. It helped us realistically predict what we were up against and not be overly optimistic that meetings or procedures would go our way. In that way, it helped us prepare and fight more effectively.

Know the law.

You have to know the law in a number of areas. You might have a lawyer to help you in this regard generally or with regard to certain technical areas, but relying on your lawyer can be expensive. Also, there are good reasons that you may need working knowledge of the relevant statutes. Whether or not you have a lawyer, you are well served to read and copy all pertinent statutes and ordinances. It is likely that you, not your lawyer, will be attending most of the meetings and having most of the contact with people who control the process, such as village clerks and government officials. There will be applicable law in various areas, such as:

1. There is a process by which statutorily permitted petitions for zoning change, variance, or conditional use go through local government. Zoning laws may specifically state what is a permitted or non-permitted use. A proposed development may not have the proper zoning, which means a zoning change would be re-

quired before developers could legally proceed. Zoning changes typically require specific procedures, including public notice, required meetings and decisions in certain time periods, and a public hearing. Some proposed uses are consistent with the zoning scheme but may require a variance or conditional-use approval. Typically, there are separate procedures for each of those approvals.

2. For zoning changes, there may be a right of protest for neighboring landowners.

3. If annexation is an issue, there may be state laws on this, as well as local laws from both the annexing entity and the entity losing the land to be annexed.

4. If a subdivision is proposed, there may be detailed ordinances and standards, including site planning, setbacks, and other specific requirements.

5. In some instances, certain county setback and other land-use requirements may apply to government units within the county. For shoreline development in the Village of Cleveland, land annexed after a certain date follows county rules, and land annexed before that date follows village rules. This is an esoteric but critical distinction when looking at proposed development along Lake Michigan. Some towns in the county have their own zoning ordinances, whereas others rely on county statutes. And the county has overlay jurisdiction for all development within 1,000 feet of the shoreline for non-incorporated units within the county.

6. There may be state laws regulating shoreline, wetland, farmland, or other special types of land.

7. An environmental impact statement may be required, or there may be federal requirements for certain kinds of development.

If all this sounds complex and overwhelming, it is! At the least, keep to the basics. Make sure you know what procedure your governmental entity is required to follow. You'd be surprised how often local officials either do not know or deliberately ignore the law. Although you may be asking some hard questions at meetings or elsewhere, it is hard for anyone to attack you publicly if your stated position is that you want to follow the law.

You can get lots of information for free by asking.

Several issues may be obvious when you get started. If annexation or rezoning is an issue, get a copy of the current ordinances concerning those items. However, it is likely that you may not know what issues to address and may be unsure of how to get started. I recommend that you talk to people with experience and expertise in land-use issues. People will educate you, raise issues you have not considered, and suggest other avenues of research. These people can refer you to other experts and can suggest written materials as well. These resources may include statutes and ordinances, policy statements, articles, newsletters, clippings, books, and research studies.

There is no such thing as a stupid question.

I've never been shy, and I have confidence that I am intelligent. Accordingly, I have no qualms about asking people questions about anything. Perhaps some of that comes from the early days of my career as a litigator when I took a lot of depositions. It is amazing the answers you get when you ask the questions. That experience cured me of assuming that I knew the answer to a question, and of assuming that someone else understood better than I did. Be bold. As you gather information, you will also gather confidence and your questions will become more sophisticated. Once you are informed, you will be armed to defend your point intelligently at all opportunities.

People like to help.

If someone doesn't want to help you, they won't take your call, or they will be short with you when you do call. Don't take this personally. In my experience, this rarely or never happens. For the most part, people are eager to share their knowledge and expertise and to help people trying to save land or fight local government. A developer or government official might be snide at a meeting or try to make points in public at your expense. But you will be treated respectfully when you ask an expert for some advice or education. Most people relish the opportunity to share their knowledge with you simply because you are interested enough to ask.

How do I get started?

How do you go about information gathering? Make a list of the issues you can identify. The list will change and grow as you get further into the process, but it's a good starting point. With Fischer Creek, the list got increasingly long and complex. We started with a few issues:

1. Annexation of town land into the village.
2. Tax consequences of upscale residential development.
3. Economic costs of upscale residential development.
4. Effects of such a development on the quality of life in the village.
5. Who stands to benefit from the development; who stands to be hurt by the development.

As we progressed, additional issues surfaced:

6. Cost of the village's putting in a new wastewater treatment plant.
7. Calculation of whether and how much a new development would assist in lowering sewer and water bills.
8. Costs of unfunded environmental mandates.
9. Relationship between the state's anti-sprawl reports and the state's clean-water mandates.
10. Politics between the village's current leadership and various factions of frustrated citizens.
11. Taxation, state taxes, school taxes, revenue share, and how they would be affected by adding development.
12. Calculation of sewer and water rates and the effects of development on current utility usage and future excess capacity.
13. Fish and wildlife management, and the "edge effect" of development on habitat.

As we progressed even further and put forth an alternate vision for the land, we got into issues such as:

14. History of state and county efforts to buy the land as a park.
15. Raising money to buy the land as a park.
16. Requirements of the state stewardship fund for conservation purchases.
17. County politics regarding getting assistance in the form of finan-

cial contribution toward the purchase of Fischer Creek and/or management of the land as a park.

Cast a wide net.

Lots of people have expertise with regard to these issues. As you talk to people, some of them may become partners in your effort by allowing you to use their name, writing letters on your behalf, attending meetings, or otherwise helping. Be creative and don't be shy about whom you call to ask questions. Throughout the fight for Fischer Creek, I talked to many people:

1. Professors at the University of Wisconsin in Madison and in Milwaukee about urban sprawl, urban planning, rural planning, and the economics of development. Dr. Jack Huddleston became an important partner and traveled to Cleveland to conduct an educational planning seminar for village officials.
2. State employees in Madison in the Department of Administration about the state's review process for annexation petitions.
3. State employees in Madison at the Department of Natural Resources about any state conservation review requirements for shoreline development and the availability of state stewardship funds for purchase of the land.
4. State employees at the Department of Natural Resources in Green Bay about application and qualification for stewardship funds and as a source of expertise in specific areas, such as stream bank setbacks, trout stream classification, and other wildlife-management matters. The DNR community liaison in Green Bay, Jeff Pagels, became a key member of our team to conserve Fischer Creek. Jeff appeared at a Cleveland Plan Commission meeting and provided enormous help throughout the process of purchasing the land and all that that entailed. He also became our advocate within the DNR for the project.
5. The Wisconsin state intervenor, Kathleen Falk, about whether her office could support our efforts in some way. (The answer was "no.")
6. Numerous not-for-profit conservation organizations, to learn if they could help, to find out who else had done what we were

doing, to get names of other people who might assist us, and to rely on them as a source for background materials on the environment and the effects of development. Later, we asked some of these same organizations for letters of support.

7. Citizens from within Wisconsin and other states who had fought similar battles and dealt with similar issues. Through word of mouth and networking, you start to learn about others. Some people called me after learning about our efforts. More often than not, people were looking for help *from* us. But everyone offered personal experience that added to our understanding.

8. Lawyers in Wisconsin and from Chicago, where the developer was from, who understood the legal and economic basis for organizing a development of this sort. Their input was key to formulating our strategy. We learned how important speed is to a developer putting together a development, how much developers are leveraged, what their typical tactics for getting a proposal through local government were, and under what circumstances they would cut out. This provided tremendous information to help us devise our strategy.

9. Developers, who supplied similar information about the process of development.

10. Professional planners, who discussed what is considered good and cutting-edge development, explained the economics of development for the developer and the village, and offered creative ideas for development on this kind of site. For example, we learned about cluster development, a new design idea that preserves open land. We used that concept to counter the developer's plan and offer an alternative that we viewed as acceptable. We learned about how environmentally sensitive developments are actually planned and constructed, debunking the developer's claim that his was an "environmentally sensitive" plan. The Fischer Creek developer had never even consulted a landscape architect until well into the Cleveland approval process, when we forced him to reduce proposed density and defend the environmental sensitivity of his plans. We learned how to calculate the costs of development to the village. We stated

with authority that village officials had no idea whatsoever what the real economic costs were going to be.

11. Government regional planners, who supplied information on what else had been done in the region as well as on the political and legal climate of these matters.

12. Former village officials and plan commission members, who discussed the political currents in the village and the political background to the issues.

13. Engineers, who discussed the economics of new wastewater treatment plants and the political climate for these mandates. This information enabled us to show that many communities were facing what Cleveland was facing in terms of a new wastewater treatment plant. They also helped us calculate the dollar impact of new construction on a current household's sewer and water bill. This information enabled us to quantify a nebulous argument. Those favoring the development stated, "We will have lower water bills." We quantified the argument, asserting, "If every unit in the development is built and occupied, there will be less than three dollars per month difference on the average household's bill." We could then offset that amount with the costs that would be incurred, both financially and in terms of the quality of life.

14. You or your group will probably need your own counsel at some point in this process. But even before that happens, you can learn a lot by calling lawyers and asking about representation. Lawyers will frequently give you a lot of good background information if you call and inquire generally about representation. Lawyers can also point you to other people, such as government officials, and to reference materials within and outside the law.

15. The village clerk can be your best friend. He or she has access to all the local ordinances and sometimes is a living repository of village history and lore. She or he also knows when meetings will occur and what the agendas are, and has the meeting packets, as well as copies of submissions from the developer. Be very nice to the village clerk.

16. In Wisconsin, the county keeps tax records and deeds. County

employees can help you find out who really owns the land (developers may represent that they own land when in fact they do not); they can help you find out if the land is in arrears. They are sitting on a wonderful cache of dry but potentially helpful information. In Fischer Creek, for example, one of the two Chicago developers had previously purchased land in Cleveland. We learned that he owed more than $10,000 in taxes on land in the village and county and had not paid taxes for the past two years. The developer claimed it was an "oversight" and blamed his lawyers. Of course it was no oversight. He was so leveraged that he paid just enough taxes each year to keep his land from foreclosure. This helped open the eyes of some people in the village about the real practices of some developers.

17. Local historians, who told us the history of the bridge at Fischer Creek, explained the use of the land as a military route in the last century, and described other historical features of the land. This information adds color and drama to a dry discussion.

18. Local Native American experts, who discussed the location of burial mounds in the area and other aspects of the land important to Native Americans.

Don't take anything at face value.

The paradox of talking to all these people is that you learn not to believe anything just because someone tells you—especially information from the developer or officials of a hostile local government. As you talk to people and start to read, you will come to recognize when you are told lies, and when there are inconsistencies between what you are told and what you read. You will come to learn who has credibility and in what areas. You will come to be an expert and to know more about the topic than anyone else. This can lead to a lot of frustration because no one else will treat you as an expert. Other people will be seen as having more credibility simply because they are the developer or because they hold an office or title. Nonetheless, keep at it. The knowledge base will be invaluable throughout the process and may come to help you when you least expect it.

CHAPTER TWO

GET INVOLVED

(One Person Can Do a Lot)

A developer in cahoots with local government may seem like insurmountable opposition. But I assure you—one person can do a lot to thwart the machine of development because we are also a society that gives rights to individuals.

As a citizen, you have the right to the free exchange of information.

Most public meetings have public input sessions at which you have the right to speak.

As a resident, you may have the right to public hearings on certain matters before your government.

As a neighboring landowner, you may have the right to be notified of proposed activities and to protest certain actions by filing a formal protest.

You have the right to have your government conduct open meetings and to be given notice of those meetings.

You have the right to review and copy documentation considered by government in making decisions.

You have the right to be represented by counsel.

You have the right to petition your government for a redress of grievances.

You have the right to assemble and to hold meetings of your own.

You have the right to talk to a free press.

Will it be hard work? Yes. Will it be expensive? Maybe. But an individual who knows her rights and exercises them can be formidable opposition to the machine of development.

You're not alone.

While you can be effective on your own, take comfort in the knowledge that you will not have to be alone for long. The act of stepping forward to speak, to question, to learn, will create an environment in which other people start coming forward. It may be other frustrated citizens; it may be government employees who do not like what is going on; it may be elected officials. It may take an ongoing effort to organize and use this support most effectively, but you will begin to find a group of like-minded individuals as soon as you get involved. It is the actions of one or two concerned individuals that start movement and create momentum.

The "point man" (or woman)

Even as other people start to get involved, it is the continuous and concerted actions of one or a few individuals that determine success. It takes enormous energy and commitment on the part of a few people to keep everyone informed, get them to meetings, get them writing letters, delegate important tasks, and sustain the energy and interest.

One or two people will naturally become the focal point for receiving and giving information. It will happen informally at first. For example, you will get calls because someone heard you speak at a meeting or learned from someone else that you know what is going on. You will make calls to gather information, and people will start calling you back. Depending on how big the issue becomes and how many people get involved, a small group of individuals may develop as "point man" each within their own area of expertise. For Fischer Creek, Rolf Johnson was the expert on scientific matters, I handled legal and economic concerns, and John Kirsch handled local politics, planning, and design issues. Soon you will be communicating with your other "point men" and sharing information. Behold! A leadership circle is born!

Exactly what can I do?

A lot!

1. Start with gathering the information described in Chapter One.
2. Go to public meetings and monitor what occurs, even if you do not participate. Government officials act different when they know they are being watched.
3. Go to meetings and speak up. Let them know there is citizen concern and dissent.
4. Lobby your local officials. Whether it is board, plan commission, or committee, call members and talk to them. Express your concerns. Sometimes this helps in unexpected ways. Some officials will be sympathetic to you, but they need ammunition in the form of your support and information in order to take a public stand in a meeting.
5. Assert that you know your legal rights as a citizen and insist on them.
6. Write letters to appropriate officials.
7. Inform your fellow citizens by distributing leaflets, writing letters to the editor, making calls, and circulating petitions.
8. Challenge the statements of the developer and government officials whenever they are inaccurate. They will be wrong a lot, whether about such matters as what the law states, the proper procedure to be followed, or the economic consequences of their decision.
9. Raise money.
10. Hire a lawyer.
11. Notify the press.
12. Call your own meetings.
13. Serve as a board, commission, or committee member.

What resources are needed?

Take your vitamins. The main resources you need are your own time and energy. None of what has to be done is rocket science. It is all eminently doable by an ordinary motivated citizen. What it takes is a huge amount of effort. Some people have commented that the leadership circle of Fischer Creek was highly unusual because we had so many credentials. I had a legal and business management background; Rolf was a scientist with extensive fund-raising and media experience; John was an architect and planner; Donny was a wastewater engineer. Perhaps we were extraordinary, but I don't think so. If anything was extraordinary, it was our commitment, not our credentials. If that's the case, then every community has extraordinary people who can come forward when the situation requires. Don't get discouraged. Keep at it.

What motivates you?

Now may be a good time to think about what motivates you. Is it your passion for the out-of-doors? Your love of birding? Your protective instincts for all the critters that will be displaced by this loss of habitat? Your anger at outside interests controlling your quality of life and your community? Your frustration with local government's making one too many boneheaded decisions? It does not matter whether your personal motivation is love or anger. You will need a strong motivator, whatever it is, to keep you going. It is this motivator that enables ordinary people to do extraordinary things.

My motivator changed over time, and changed from project to project. For Fischer Creek, my initial motivator was that I was angry at the power of a few "good old boys" in the village, who thought they were not accountable to the voters. I was also intensely frustrated that village officials were about to make a huge decision, by all definitions a *material* decision about the future of the village, and they had no objective information about the consequences of the decision. It offended me as someone with extensive business planning experience.

At the first plan commission meeting I attended, the developer more or less said, "There's nothing you can do about stopping the development. It's progress, and besides it will be good for you." I was livid! When the developer, the village president, and the chairman of the plan commission all assumed "there's nothing you can do about it," my natural inclination was to say, "Oh, yes, there is." And we did. This is still a democracy, and the voters still have some control over the actions of their elected officials. I learned that exercising the rights of a citizen in a democracy is harder and more time-consuming than I imagined. The lawmakers have weighted the system in their favor, and most of the time the system just grinds on. But once in a while, the democratic system works. That's what you have to work for.

I was also motivated by my lifelong inclination to support the underdog. In this case, the "underdog" was the citizens of Cleveland who were being steamrollered by their own government. I met a group of citizens at the first plan commission meeting who were frustrated and did not know what to do. I like to help people empower themselves.

Another element in my motivation, unfortunately for the developer, was that I had just left a career in Chicago's options and futures markets, which is an extremely macho and male-dominated world. I had pretty much reached my limit for tolerating cocky, young, white guys playing "Master of the Universe." Mr. Fogelson, the developer, reminded me too much of what I had just left. I had not given up my career and moved to Wisconsin only to be caught in the same dynamic. He pushed my buttons.

As we progressed and I learned more about the topography, habitat, and history of Fischer Creek, and about the history of land stewardship in Wisconsin, I became motivated by conservation concerns as well. I wanted to preserve rather than destroy. I had chosen Cleveland as an alternative to the city and was loathe to see it citified even before my boxes were unpacked. One development does not make a city, but more than most people in Cleveland, I knew who would be buying luxurious second homes on Lake Michigan—my old colleagues from LaSalle Street. I wanted a quiet life in a rural community with habitat for birds, and I was prepared to fight to keep Cleveland that way.

My final motivator was that I do not suffer fools gladly. As we got into the facts and the truths, it became obvious to me that the development was being promoted by people who had absolutely no idea what the real consequences would be. They had no facts, and their attitude was "My mind is made up, don't confuse me with the facts." Sometimes, if something is just stupid enough, you have to stop it.

Clear the kitchen table.

What you are setting out to do is difficult. It can also be exhilarating. It is something that any citizen can do—if motivated enough. Developers develop for a living. They have lawyers, public relations experts, and capital at their disposal. You are doing this in addition to your full-time commitments, whether they include a job, running a household, caring for family members young and old, community service, or other aspects of a full life you care about. That is one of the basic inequities of the struggle. Developing is what a developer does. For you, fighting development is added on top of everything else you already do. The developer has an office. You have the kitchen table.

During the early months of Fischer Creek, I ate countless dinners at the home of my neighbors, John and Idell Kirsch. John came home from a full day at work, and we met night after night, as well as on weekends. I don't know how he did it. We joked about their putting my picture on the wall because I was living there more than their daughter. We kept the Chinese take-out place in business. John wanted one and only one dish: lobster egg fu young. To this day, the mere whiff of lobster egg fu young sends me back to 1994 and their living room sofa. John and Idell didn't have a kitchen table. The sofa served as the all-points meeting ground.

What other resources will you need?

Other invaluable resources are basic: e-mail, telephone, and a fax machine. In terms of information gathering, fax and e-mail are critical. If people want to send you information, typically one of these two methods will work, except for lengthy documents or statutes. When we began work on Fischer Creek, I bought a fax machine but did not have e-mail. Now I can't imagine working on a land battle without e-mail. By the time of Point Creek, I communicated mostly by e-mail, with telephone a distant second. You should proceed with whatever resource is most comfortable. I have an inclination for e-mail, because it is the fastest and most efficient way to communicate information and inform people about meetings. Not everyone has e-mail, however, and I sometimes found myself not communicating at all with people I had to phone. I should probably pick up the phone more often and talk to people. E-mail is no substitute for the relationship building that occurs when you talk.

Telephone is critical not only for establishing and building relationships, but for discussing strategy or complex issues. When you are building a coalition, people need personal contact to get them involved and keep them involved. E-mail is more efficient for transmitting specific pieces of information—meeting times, news updates, things of that nature. E-mail works for curt, business-like communications and can be more efficient than calling a bunch of people with the same piece of information. Also, it is more efficient than playing telephone tag, which wastes time. Depending on with whom you are communicating, e-mail helps keep "talkers" from letting you use your time efficiently. Of course, e-mail is only of use in reaching people who have it and check it regularly, so it will never replace the telephone.

For dealing with governmental agencies or grant authorities, e-mail is often faster and is a good supplement to a personal and telephone relationship. Some grants require electronic submissions and do not handle paper applications anymore. E-mail is also a great way to circulate documents. We share press clippings largely by e-mail, for example. Someone finds an article and sends the link to interested parties. E-mail also works well for documents that need to be reviewed by several people.

A lot of documents are still not in electronic format, so fax works for those. A fax is especially good for obtaining documents that have been submitted to a local or regional unit of government, meeting packets, land registrar information, and local ordinances. Sometimes you have to get these documents in person and pay for copying. But if you have a relationship with an employee, and if the documents are not lengthy, a village clerk or county employee may throw it on the fax for you. This saves you time and energy.

Take personal responsibility for the project.

Whether or not you hire a lawyer, build a coalition, or forge partnerships, ultimately it is the responsibility of one or a few individuals to gather information and determine how to use it. You cannot assume someone else will do it (unless you have made specific allocations of responsibility and you know that the task will in fact get done). My basic assumption was always that if I wanted something done, I had to do it myself. It is a lot of work and a lot of responsibility. It is also a lot of power.

Following are examples of the kinds of materials I tracked down for the Point Creek project and how I ultimately used the materials. You may find a lot of this material useful for future land-use issues in your community.

1. *Developer submission to county requesting variance for Point Creek.* We saw the layout of the proposed subdivision, the density, and the proposed setbacks. We knew the extent of the development threat and used that to garner support for conservation. Several individuals went to the variance hearing at the county plan commission and voiced strong objections, based in part on some of the materials described below. Those citizens succeeded in getting the variance approval delayed for two meetings, which slowed the developer's momentum and gave us time to begin organization, publicity, and fund-raising efforts. They also learned that the Town of Centerville supported the development because it wanted the tax base.

2. *Current county shoreline setback requirements.* We used these for a number of purposes: We assessed the practicality of the developer's plans for Point Creek based on the setbacks. We also used the setbacks to assess the fair market value of the land, should we enter into negotiations for purchase of the land. The setbacks would also have proved useful for monitoring building permits in the event that we had to fight a specific development proposed for the site. We met with the county building inspector on site at Point Creek, walked the required setbacks for homes, and learned of the likelihood of variances being granted to move homes closer to the shore (not likely).

3. *Proposed new county shoreline setback requirements.* We learned the status of proposed new county setback requirements that are more stringent than the current requirements. We used this information to assess the market value of land and the effects of delays, which could force the developer to comply with the

new setback requirements. This also gave us insight into where the county was headed (toward more, not less, regulation of shoreline development), which helped us assess the likelihood of future variances being given for site planning and construction.

4. *Study of the Coastal Wetlands of Manitowoc County.* The county commissioned this study from the University of Wisconsin in Madison, using a grant from the Wisconsin Coastal Management Program. The study delineates important and scarce natural features of Point Creek. This provided a scientific basis for conservation of this particular parcel. While we did not prevent the county from granting the developer's request for a variance, we were able to delay consideration of the variance, in part by citing scientific studies about the land. This study was also critical in our efforts to raise funds from both private sources and government. The Wisconsin Coastal Management Program also had money available for purchase of property along the Great Lakes. It favors funding projects that implement previous planning work, especially previous planning work funded by them. We ultimately obtained an $800,000 grant from Wisconsin Coastal Management Program to purchase Point Creek, and this study was an important factor in getting the grant.

5. *Joint Land Use Plan, Town of Centerville and Village of Cleveland.* The Joint Land Use Plan designated environmental corridors, including Point Creek. We now had a planning foundation for conserving the land. Wisconsin Coastal Management Program also funded the Joint Land Use Plan, and we emphasized that point in our grant application to them.

6. *Wisconsin Department of Natural Resources Land Legacy Study.* I heard references to this study and found it on the department's Web site. It showed that the department had designated Point Creek a priority area. This helped our applications for both departmental and Wisconsin Coastal Management Program grants, and also helped our credibility as we sought funds from private sources.

7. *Biological Inventory of Kingfisher Farm.* The University of Wisconsin in Green Bay conducted this study for a piece of land, Kingfisher Farm, which adjoins Point Creek to the south. The in-

ventory showed a vast range of plants and wildlife on the King-fisher Farm parcel. We used it as further scientific evidence in our fund-raising, as well as for eventually securing UW Green Bay as a partner in the project. People are more inclined to give money if they can relate to something about the cause. In our case, the biological inventory identified numerous birds, mammals, and plants, in addition to the large population of great blue herons already identified with the site.

8. *Real estate agent for developer's previous attempt to sell the land.* A neighboring landowner to Point Creek, Ron Schaper, re-membered that Point Creek had been for sale some years back. Ron tracked down the name of the real estate firm, found the individual who had worked on the listing, and received useful insights about pricing and the developer's business style. When Point Creek was listed for sale, the real estate company, which had made a large investment, ultimately abandoned its efforts because the landowner would not budge on price. Learning about this gave us insight into the landowner's style and meth-ods, and helped us realistically predict his response to our price negotiations.

I could go on, but you can see how one or two people can gather im-portant information. There is power and authority in putting all the information together and looking at it as a whole. It takes only one individual to track down important material, read it, and figure out how to use it.

Sorting through disinformation

As a grassroots effort takes off, an active rumor mill often accompa-nies it. Lots of people become involved peripherally and hear things far removed from the source. Also, at least in the smaller commu-nities that I have observed, changing land use seems to engender gossip. Land use is personal and emotional. It promotes strong feel-ings and reactions. People talk about and respond to what they hear without ascertaining the underlying facts. Lots of "information" is passed around, much of it silly, wrong, or misguided. People will tell you things with absolute authority that turn out to be untrue. Usually there is an individual who is on top of the latest, best information, who can guide people and advise as to next steps.

Rotating leadership

Individuals make things happen. In a particularly long or difficult land fight, you will be lucky if you have a small group of individuals who can rotate into and out of leadership positions. This keeps things going when different skills are needed, when someone is burned out and needs a rest, or when someone has to step back due to other life commitments.

The leadership circle for Fischer Creek

For Fischer Creek, we were blessed with rotating leadership. Although we ultimately built momentum for a big grassroots coalition, with partners in government and conservation organizations, it was really the concerted work of a few individuals that made it all happen.

I was heavily involved throughout. My role was to gather and absorb huge amounts of information, figuring out how to use the information effectively, hiring lawyers and working closely with them, devising strategy, providing a business and economic viewpoint on the effects of the proposed development, speaking at meetings, giving interviews to reporters, writing letters to the editor, and organizing community support.

Rolf Johnson provided a positive vision for conservation, a scientific basis for our position, and was our main face for the media. He also had excellent connections in government and the private conservation community, which were useful in raising money and enlisting partners. Rolf also began to videotape meetings for a documentary about the fight for Fischer Creek. Having the camera there may have tempered some of the behaviors of an increasingly frustrated political old guard. Rolf was highly effective at turning the eyes of the world to what was happening in Cleveland.

John Kirsch was a longtime resident and former plan commission member who knew and understood local politics. John himself designs and manages development projects. He offered expertise on all aspects of project design, landscape design, and the development process, and educated all of us as to how things are done, what this particular developer was and was not doing, and what proposals based on principles of good design and planning might look like. John offered day-to-day guidance on dealing with local officials and set the tone of our protest so that we would reach, rather than alienate, the citizens. John also was the main contributor to our alternative land-use plan, based on preservation of quality of life and community values. Finally, John agreed to run for the village board and serve on that body if elected, thereby giving us a voice inside the system.

Don Pirrung is an engineer and offered expertise on the costs of wastewater plants and the projected costs to residents of the proposed development. Also, Don spearheaded the fight to get a referendum on the ballot. I thought a referendum was a good idea but frankly was too exhausted to organize it myself. Don and I shared responsibility. I worked with our lawyers on the legality and wording of the referendum. Don did all the work of organizing the petition drive, the community outreach, and our campaign of supporting a write-in candidate to unseat the village president and several candidates to sit on the village board.

Many, many other individuals contributed in numerous ways, and Fischer Creek would not have happened without them—the ladies who circulated petitions door to door, countless citizens who attended meetings and spoke, donors of money and services, friends who hosted parties, supporters who wrote songs and donated original art, local businesses that donated banking services, mailings, printing, and photocopies from their facilities, residents who displayed posters and lawn signs, children who distributed leaflets, and everyone who voted. My point is that we were successful because *individuals* took action, providing continuity and leadership in the large grassroots coalition.

One neighbor stopped a condominium development.

Perhaps the most inspiring story of what one person can do is the story of Hika Conservancy. When developers proposed condominiums for the land adjoining Hika Park, many people opposed the development. Residents of the Hika neighborhood and others wanted to add the conservancy land to the park. In terms of development, the community wanted single-family homes, which would be consistent with the existing land-use plans and zoning, as well as with the character of the historic Hika neighborhood. Some village board members, however, were looking for an increased tax base for the village as a whole, even though the neighborhood clearly opposed condominiums.

However, it was essentially one couple who stopped the development. Otto and Laurel Wimpffen are my next-door neighbors. The Hika Conservancy land is their next-door neighbor on their southern property line. Quiet, gentle people who bought their cottage for its peaceful setting, the Wimpffens plan on retiring to their cottage in Cleveland in a few years. Like their other neighbors, they relied on existing zoning—which prohibits multifamily development—when buying their property and planning for the future.

As we initially investigated the developer's proposal for condominium development, we learned that the Cleveland ordinances were complex and outdated. We soon identified a number of technical issues related to the petition and appropriate procedure that the ordinances did not address. We also learned that as contiguous neighboring property owners, the Wimpffens had a right to protest a zoning change and could force the board to approve a zoning change only if a three-quarters supermajority voted in its favor. Finally, we learned that most of the board was in favor of the zoning change and condominium development.

It became obvious that the Wimpffens needed legal help to fight the proposed development properly. They bit the bullet and hired a lawyer. It cost them a lot of money, but with counsel, they succeeded in their fight against the proposed condominiums and petition for rezoning. (I will give more details of that struggle in later chapters.) Ultimately, the developers asked the village to table the rezoning petition for an unspecified period and to buy the land from them for a village park.

The village is taking steps to purchase Hika Conservancy, and their success may take several more years. However, even if Cleveland cannot raise the $530,000 needed to purchase the parcel, the worst-case scenario is likely to see a few single-family homes, not condominiums.

While the Wimpffens fought the legalities of the rezoning, other neighbors provided support by attending meetings, writing letters defending preservation of the character of the neighborhood, and maintaining that the village as a whole would benefit from public ownership of the sand beach and wetlands adjoining Hika Park. Several board members strongly advocated for conservation of the land during plan commission and village board meetings. But despite the strong public sentiment against the development, it was mostly the legal research and threat of litigation that stopped the development. In Hika, one couple, their lawyer, and a handful of individuals stopped a thirty-six-unit condominium development.

If that isn't a role model for success, I don't know what is!

"Cheshire Puss," she (Alice) began . . .
*"would you please tell me which way I
ought to go from here?"*
*"That depends on where you want to
get to,"* said the cat.   Lewis Carroll

DEVISE A STRATEGY
(Which Way Should We Go?)

One of the most important things you can do is devise a strategy. A strategy provides structure and direction as you decide how to spend your time and where to use your limited resources. A strategy will help you decide what to do and what not to do. There are many reasons that we succeeded, against all odds, in our fight for Fischer Creek, but I am convinced that one of the most important was that I devised a strategy and we stuck to it.

Don't confuse your ultimate goal with your strategy.

Saving land, creating a park, stopping development—these are all worthy goals. However, they are not your strategy. Your strategy is the specific way you will go about achieving your ultimate goal. Once you determine your strategy, you will then take a number of actions to implement your strategy.

Devising a strategy for Fischer Creek.
Strategy One: Get three "no" votes.

For Fischer Creek, our goal was to stop the housing development. Subsequently, our ultimate goal was to save the land for a public park. We knew that the developer needed annexation to the Village of Cleveland in order to build a development of the size and density he was proposing. Upon researching the annexation laws, we learned that annexation requires a supermajority of the board in favor of annexation. Translated, that meant we needed three "no" votes on annexation.

Strategy Two: Delay.

It was also apparent that the developer, along with village officials, were in a big rush to annex the land as fast as possible. Whenever someone is in a big rush, I get suspicious about what they are trying to cover up. What's out there that they do not want us to discover? I was convinced that with more time, information helpful to our cause and detrimental to the developer would emerge. It was also apparent that we needed time to build grassroots support and momentum to defeat the annexation. I concluded that the more time we had, the more likely we could turn information and momentum to our favor.

Strategy Three: Raise the $1.3 million purchase price for the land from the state and the county, or make significant progress in that regard, over the next four months.

Even if annexation were defeated, the ordinances permitted a landowner to refile a petition for annexation after a 120-day waiting period. Given the community's strong sentiment in favor of landowner rights, and given the economic pressures on the village because of the new multimillion-dollar wastewater treatment plant, we concluded that we needed an alternate plan for the land. We could not delay annexation forever, facing repeated annexation votes, if the land were just sitting there. Our only realistic hope for permanently defeating development was to purchase the land for conservation. Given the amount of money needed and the short time frame, we looked to government. The state and county had shown a lot of interest through the years, but negotiations always seemed to fizzle. We had to push the Department of Natural Resources and county to get their act together and buy the parcel as a park.

John, Rolf, and I wrote and presented to the community a Community Vision and Land Use Plan, which showed this land as preserved. But the village board would not indefinitely postpone annexation on the strength of a pipedream. We had a short time in which to "put up or shut up" on acquisition of Fischer Creek. We needed substantial progress in the next four months to show the board that conservation of Fischer Creek was a real possibility.

Focus on your strategy.

As a grassroots movement takes off, it is uncontrollable to a certain extent. Persons get involved, each with their own point of view, each with a different ax to grind, each with a unique style, personalized interests, and his or her own take on the situation. Getting the group to move in unison is like trying to get a pack of cats to run uphill together: It won't happen. As people are going off in all directions, focus on your strategy.

During Fischer Creek, Rolf Johnson talked about habitat and the coastal watershed to anyone who would listen and gave speeches on how ecology and economics come from the same Greek root. Rolf created a vision of a biological island encompassing an area much larger than Fischer Creek. The media loved Rolf, and he got us the most publicity. That in itself built credibility and momentum for the Friends of Fischer Creek. Rolf was also the best fund-raiser and was important in getting appraisals done on the land and getting donations to pay for those appraisals.

John Kirsch preached a vision for protecting our quality of life in Cleveland. His thoughts were community-related and reflected on why people choose to make their homes here. John caused people to be concerned that their quality of life was threatened. He also focused on making the developer responsible for the effects of the development. His letters and questions in this regard were important in sowing doubt about the consequences of the annexation. Also, John knew the plan commission and board members. He provided the most insight into what would positively and negatively affect their votes and thus became a key person in deciding what actions we should take.

I preached economic responsibility and encouraged the village to use a rational process for making the annexation decision. Also, I worked closely with our lawyer to make sure that the village followed every procedural requirement. I advocated delay so that the board and plan commission could take time to answer questions and engage in appropriate analysis of the consequences of annexation. And through the lawyers, we were making sure that the board delayed the process at least to the extent required by law.

Many other people came to meetings, spoke, circulated petitions, wrote letters, and wanted to participate. We had as many viewpoints and ideas as people involved. One of my self-appointed tasks was to take all this activity and funnel it, as best possible, toward our strategy. How could we focus this activity to increase the likelihood of delay? How could we focus this activity to increase the likelihood of getting three "no" votes?

With time, the focus became even narrower. We knew we had one "no" vote for certain. After a time, we were relatively confident of a second. We had one board member who had not declared herself (even to her husband, who worked with John). Ultimately we focused on her. How could we convince Julie Furmanski to vote no?

The process of fighting for Fischer Creek was not tidy. We were constantly getting new information from many sources: substantive information on the costs of development, models for making development decisions, planning reports, political intelligence, community actions and reactions. Reporters sought information and interviews, and local papers published articles one or more times a week. But amid this seemingly chaotic activity, I always remembered the strategy: three "no" votes. I reminded myself and everyone else: We need three "no" votes. As people proposed a variety of actions and strategies, I asked: Would this delay approval? Would it help convince three trustees to vote "no"? We needed the delay to get the three "no" votes. We needed three "no" votes to defeat the annexation. We needed to defeat the annexation to defeat the development.

After several months of intense activity, I concluded that if we wanted to defeat development of the site permanently, we also had to raise money to purchase the land for a park. From that point on, we spent a lot of energy seeking the $1.3 million to purchase the land and meeting the requirements of the DNR Stewardship Fund. It was tough to run two strategies simultaneously, working on defeat of the annexation vote *and* funding the purchase price. We knew that if we lost the annexation vote, all our efforts at fund-raising would have been wasted. But we needed significant progress on the park issue to avoid losing a second annexation vote, which could occur as soon as four months after the first vote. It was a gamble we had to take.

We met with representatives of the DNR, and our DNR community liaison from Green Bay, Jeff Pagels, attended a plan commission meeting to discuss the fact that there might be money for the purchase of Fischer Creek in the stewardship fund. Jeff's appearance let the community know that conservation was not a pipedream and that it really was possible to buy the land as a park. We were doing everything we could to sow seeds of doubt in the minds of the village board about the merits of annexation, in the hopes that three trustees would vote "no."

Determine your implementation steps.

Once you have a strategy, then you can decide on a variety of implementation actions. Let's take our first strategy, delay—a strategy that fits many situations. What can you do to delay the process? Hire a lawyer, for one. More on that later, but the main point is: When have lawyers ever speeded up a process?

During Fischer Creek, another tactic we used to cause a delay was to ask, "What don't we know?" We wanted to make local officials afraid to act quickly. We raised numerous questions and thereby created doubt in what had been a clear picture painted by the developer. Suddenly this picture of beautiful development bringing mounds of cash into the village had all manner of potential problems. What would services cost? What services would we have to provide? What would traffic patterns look like? Would our streets be unsafe for kids to play in? What comes into a community when money arrives? Drugs? Speeding? What else? What are the assumptions about tax revenues? Has anyone questioned them? What about the research that shows that tax revenues never meet expenses? What will happen to the Class I trout stream? Are there any controls in place for avoiding its pollution? I could go on and on, but you get the idea. You never know what question or issue will resonate with a trustee. The important thing was not to have an answer to every question. The important point is that the very asking of the question implements your strategy of delay.

At the same time, we presented the plan commission, village

board, and community with an alternate vision for a park and a land-use plan for preserving our quality of life in Cleveland. Trustees don't like to look stupid or hasty. Trustees don't want to be responsible for decisions that upset the status quo. When the developer presented his plan, it looked picture perfect. Now we were painting a picture of drugs and speeders and a divided village and no place to fish. We wanted to make it harder for the trustees to act quickly. The more doubts we raised, the more time they had to spend considering, or appearing to consider, the consequences.

It was harder to determine what steps we needed to take in order to get three "no" votes. We hoped that all our actions creating delay would also convince three trustees to vote "no" on the merits. One of the most important activities for getting three "no" votes was initiated by Don Pirrung, who strongly advocated we mount a referendum on the issue. The laws of the State of Wisconsin make it difficult for citizen referendums to succeed. Lawmakers do not want the people making laws, perhaps because then all those legislators might be superfluous. Because of the procedural and technical requirements in Wisconsin's referendum law, we faced some difficulties in getting the referendum on the ballot and then getting it passed. And it was likely that a referendum would be advisory in any event. But Don's suggestion was brilliant and may have been the decisive step in effecting our strategy of getting three "no" votes.

Because of the timing of the election, the referendum would come *after* the board vote on annexation. Therefore, we had a new rallying cry: "Let the people decide!" A "no" vote on annexation no longer meant that a trustee was voting *against* development. With a referendum scheduled for April, a "no" vote on annexation now meant a trustee was voting *for* letting the people decide. We gave the trustees a big "out" from their dilemma of making a decision. And it worked. We did get three "no" votes, and at least one of those came from a trustee who wanted to hear from the people through the electoral process.

By the way, we lost the referendum by a few votes, although it was never clear what the mandate of the people was in terms of permitting annexation or establishing the park. We could not word the referendum to say "Do you want this annexation?" or "Do you want to see Fischer Creek as a park?" State law required us to come up with wording using different concepts, and the final referendum read, "Resolved, that the Village of Cleveland shall maintain its northern boundary east of C.T.H. LS." Although it was disappointing, as it turned out, it did not matter that we lost the referendum by a few votes. By then, we had strong momentum for funding the land as a park. The referendum bought us the time we needed to make substantial progress toward making the park a reality. Should the developer or landowner return with a second petition for annexation in four months, we could show a viable alternate land use for Fischer Creek.

Be prepared to alter your strategy.

Yes, you should devise a strategy. Yes, you should stick to it. But don't be afraid to change your strategy if that makes sense given a changing situation. With Fischer Creek, we added a significant strategy after several months—raise $1.3 million to purchase the land for a park.

Our strategy changed over time in the Point Creek project as well. For the most part, Point Creek, unlike Fischer Creek, did not involve local politics. Point Creek was about raising money and convincing the landowner (who was also a developer) of our credibility as a purchaser so that he would delay bulldozing the property. Some of our success was not due to strategy but to dumb luck. I am certain that if anyone else had come along with the landowner's asking price, he would have taken it. But no one did, and that gave us time to put together a financial package.

Our strategy for Point Creek was threefold: (1) Keep the landowner at the table and delay development of the parcel or sale to anyone else; (2) raise money to purchase the land from public and private sources; and (3) gather information to be used to negotiate a lower price with the landowner.

Throughout our dealings with the landowner, he demanded $1.9 million for the parcel. This amount was significantly higher than either appraisal we received and turned out to be half a million dollars higher than the DNR-approved amount for purchase. We did considerable research into setbacks, where houses would be sited, view lines, and other shoreline-development issues, and I was personally convinced that the DNR was right and that the $1.9 million asking price was grossly inflated.

The landowner refused to budge in any negotiations. He clung to that figure of $1.9 million to the point of irrationality. The landowner had set up the negotiation as a win/lose scenario, and rejected all attempts to make it win/win. For example, he gave no credence to the time value of money (that is, that $1.9 million cash in the future is equal to less cash in hand today). He wanted $1.9 million; yet he was willing to wait three or more years for the same amount of cash under a contract. In real dollars, $1.9 million in hand is worth less than $1.9 million in three years. Yet the owner refused to negotiate based on the fact that taking a lower dollar amount up front and in cash would be financially rational for him. He also refused to consider a bargain sale, whereby his net after-tax proceeds would equal or exceed the after-tax proceeds of a $1.9 million sale. In fact, he refused to negotiate any financial aspect of the transaction. It became obvious that $1.9 million was a "magic" number for the landowner and we were in a "take it or leave it" situation.

At some point in the process, we abandoned any notion of paying a reduced price for a cash transaction and had to face the difficult decision of whether to buy the land at an inflated price or abandon our efforts. The land conservancy board decided to proceed with the effort to purchase the land, so our strategy simply became finding $1.9 million and keeping the landowner at the table while we did so.

Your strategy should influence how you proceed.

One of the benefits of having a strategy is that you can assess whether a contemplated activity is constructive, of no particular value, or perhaps hinders your ability to realize your ultimate goal. For the Hika conservation project, we had two different strategies that we had to pursue delicately in tandem. Knowing these two strategies up front helped us proceed cautiously and analyze every possible action from the vantage point of how that action would affect each strategy.

For the Hika situation, the developer proposed condominiums. In order to put condominiums on that parcel, the developers required a zoning change. Because of the potentially serious effect of a zoning change on neighbors, the village ordinances allow a right of protest for contiguous landowners. If a neighbor exercises this right of protest, then the zoning change must be approved by a super-majority of the board. In practical terms, for Hika, that meant that two "no" votes at the board level would defeat the zoning change. The Wimpffens intended to exercise their right of protest, although the timing of the protest was a matter of some strategic importance. Our ultimate goal was to have the village buy the land for a park, but we knew that some development was possible and inevitable if the developer chose to develop under the existing zoning regulations, which permitted single-family homes.

Our initial strategy for Hika was twofold. The first part of the strategy was to delay board action on the rezoning to give us enough time to ensure that we had two "no" votes if the petition for rezoning came before the board. The second part of our strategy considered the possibility that development would occur on the parcel. In that event, we wanted to get a "seat at the table" should the village be involved in site planning for development at that location. By "seat at the table" I mean that our opinion would be asked and our concerns addressed during the site-planning process.

The strategy to ensure that we had a voice in development influenced how we went about our campaign to defeat development. We had to fight the development but do so in a way that was positive, cordial, and helpful, and that ensured our continued participation in the process. Not an easy task. Because of this strategy, we bent over backward to avoid any negative publicity, to be sympathetic to the board and village employees, and to be neighborly and helpful throughout the process. The campaign had an entirely different tone from the one concerning Fischer Creek.

How you should proceed

Determining your strategy answers the question, "Which way should I go from here?" Knowing your strategy means knowing "where you want to get to." Assuming that time and money are limited resources, having a strategy can keep you from running off in the wrong direction or spinning your wheels on activities that don't get you anywhere. Take a little time at the beginning to do the following:

1. Identify one or more strategies for achieving your goal.
2. List implementation steps (actions) to achieve your strategy.
3. Also list actions that could be negative or harmful to your strategy. Don't undertake those actions, and discourage other people from undertaking them.
4. Reevaluate your strategy regularly, given the latest information and events.
5. Understand that land battles are largely reactive, time-pressured, and fought by a loosely organized (at best) group of essentially uncontrollable individuals. Cut yourself and others some slack when actual events do not live up to the model.
6. Nonetheless, stay focused on your strategy throughout the process.

CHAPTER FOUR

HIRE COUNSEL
("The First Thing We Do, Let's Kill All the Lawyers")

Lawyers are a much-maligned group, and the above quotation—a reference to a line in Shakespeare's Henry VI, Part 2 (Act 4, Scene 2)—testifies to this. Adorning posters, sweatshirts, buttons, and mugs, this call to action has probably increased sales of paraphernalia bearing the above quotation so much that it has kept public radio afloat.

What people forget is the context for this quotation. In the play, plotters sought to overthrow the government and curtail the people's civil rights. How would they accomplish this? Kill all the lawyers. Lawyers are the champions of individual rights in the face of mob rule. Lawyers are the champions of individual rights in the face of powerful interests. Lawyers are the champions of individual rights in the face of government. People who exercise power hate lawyers—at least other people's lawyers. If you are fighting development, you are fighting the powerful interests of business and government. You need a lawyer. You should rejoice if these interests want to kill your lawyer. That's the goal.

There are many reasons that you might need a lawyer at some point in your campaign. For every one of the three conservation projects discussed in this book, we needed counsel. Because each situation was different, we needed lawyers with different areas of expertise, at different times in the process, and for different reasons. We could not have succeeded in any of these efforts without having the right legal advocate at the right time in the process. It is best that you prepare the information you need to hire counsel and use your lawyer intelligently. That way, you will be ready to act when the time is right.

Things lawyers can do for you
Keeping local government on the straight and narrow

You are likely to be dealing with petitions for zoning changes, annexations, variances, or other actions of local government. There are likely to be procedural requirements regarding timing, as well as specific requirements regarding the content and format of these petitions. There may be open-meeting requirements and notice requirements. For a variety of reasons, local government may not follow all the local, county, and state statutory requirements. This may be because there are new citizens on the board or committee who have not learned the statutory requirements. Sometimes they have "always done it that way" and no one has reviewed or challenged old practices. Sometimes government officials really do want to rush a decision in favor of development and are deliberately ignoring the rules. In any event, it is often useful to have a lawyer guide you through the statutory maze.

Is it possible for a citizen to do this on his or her own? In some circumstances, yes. But land-use procedures and regulations are often complex and interactive, so you have to understand a wide array of related provisions to understand any given provision. It is easy for a lawyer to miss something, easier still for a novice. You may be well served, in situations involving a lot of technical requirements, to have a lawyer with land-use expertise review the procedural steps taken, notices published, and submissions filed, and even attend key meetings to monitor the proceedings and represent your interests.

Advocating favorable interpretations of laws

The law has many areas open to interpretation. Depending on how recently adopted and well written the statutory scheme, there may be a few or many ambiguities in the requirements for procedure and substantive compliance. The kinds of matters open to interpretation cover the range of land-use issues, such as whether a matter must come before a plan commission before a board vote; whether site planning is required before zoning is determined; whether gatherings require posting under an open-meetings statute; what kinds of submissions are sufficient to meet statutory requirements; and the time period and sequence in which voting decisions can be made. I could go on. Your counsel can advocate interpretations of the law that are favorable to your position. In this way, you begin to control the process in a way that benefits you.

Implementing your strategy

Often your lawyer can be an important tool for implementing your strategy. As discussed in Chapter Three, delay is a common strategy. Lawyers are great at prolongation and can often find procedural points, request information or documentation, or devise other strategies that will slow the process. Another strategy discussed in Chapter Three is getting a "seat at the table" to review site plans or participate in decision making. Lawyers can be knowledgeable and helpful, and generally ingratiate themselves to the local government. Small governments like to avail themselves of legal talent that they do not have to pay for. For the Hika Conservancy project, the village began to turn to the citizens' lawyer for answers to complicated procedural questions. While you might resent paying for your lawyer's time to advise the local government, in terms of long-term strategy, this could be an extremely positive development.

Threatening litigation

People do not like to be sued. Local government officials, in particular, are often extremely averse to the prospect. They fear they will look stupid, be embarrassed, and be forced to spend money on legal fees or judgments not in the budget. Few people welcome the animosity, disruption, and time that a lawsuit entails.

Developers also hate litigation. They want to make money as fast as possible, with as much certainty and as little risk as possible. They want to be able to quantify their risk. Litigation adds time, cost, and uncertainty to the process. It is often unpredictable, unquantifiable, and uncontrollable.

I do not recommend that you threaten to sue unless you mean it and you know what you are doing. However, the mere presence of counsel as a watchdog brings the unstated fear of litigation into play. And there may be circumstances in which litigation is a practical and necessary strategy for you.

Serving as your lightning rod for conflict

Parties to local land-use issues can be venomous. They can generate hostilities and tensions. Many people, myself included, are not comfortable being the target of these hostilities. It is especially difficult that these disputes occur in your community and affect your home, the place in which you seek respite from conflict and from tensions in the workplace.

Often, the acrimony of a land-use dispute can focus on your lawyer (instead of on you). Your lawyer may serve as a lightning rod for the hostilities your actions attract. The very presence of a lawyer changes the playing field and the dynamic of your land battle. A lot of the dispute may be played out in the legal arena, lawyer to lawyer. Also, your lawyer can step in and handle all or some aspects of your conflict with government or with the developer. The conflict is still there, but it is being funneled through counsel and not through you.

You can distance yourself from your own lawyer to a certain extent. That can help you maintain some face-saving peace with neighbors, who can choose to believe that it's not you, it's "the lawyers" who are stirring up trouble. While this may be a bit of "smoke and mirrors," it may also be effective in maintaining civility in your community. The lessened hostility can help you and others conserve strength for when it is needed.

Conducting negotiations for purchase of land

Even when there is not conflict or hostility, you may need a lawyer to negotiate with the landowner. If buying the land is one of your goals, you may need real estate counsel to negotiate an option or land contract and to close the transaction if you are successful. If a government agency is the ultimate purchaser, it may handle this; but it is also possible that you, in conjunction with one or more of your partners, will have to do it.

Responding to other lawyers

Developers, landowners, and governments have lawyers of their own. If lawyers for any of these interests are at the table, you will need your own counsel to protect your interests and to keep the other lawyers from bullying others to get their own way. Even if there is no lawyer present, the developer may threaten to bring his lawyer or may liberally quote legal opinions purportedly in hand. You need counsel to debunk this misinformation and neutralize this tactic.

Getting something done

Last, but certainly not least, is the need for your lawyer to get something done. The only way you can be sure something gets done is for you (meaning you, personally; your lawyer; or someone you trust on your team) to do it. Frequently questions arise that might fall into one or more bailiwicks. Examples include facts about the tax status or ownership of the parcel; information about past practices of government; and information about a similar situation elsewhere in the county. Often the information you need is something your local government, the landowner, or the county should know. While it is tempting, and often cheaper, to push the work onto someone else, the fact is that if you really need it done, you should probably do it yourself. It is frequently the case that these small factual matters become big factors in mounting and ultimately winning your campaign. Depending on such factors as the fee arrangement, your liquidity, your time, and the importance of the task, your lawyer may be the right person to handle the matter.

How to find and retain a lawyer

It should not be difficult to identify potentially suitable lawyers; some time on the telephone should do it. Do what you would do to get a referral for a doctor: Call to ask for recommendations. There are several kinds of people or places to call. You can call lawyers you know or currently retain on another matter. Who handled your house closing? For Fischer Creek, we wound up using the person and firm that had closed on my house earlier that year. It turned out that he usually handled commercial development, not house closings, and met the other criteria we established. You can also contact the local land trust; local environmental organizations, such as the local chapter of the Sierra Club; state or county officials who work in conservation; planners or architects; others in your state who have engaged in a grassroots development battle; friends or other sympathetic people in the community—you'd be amazed how many people have a niece or nephew working for a high-powered law firm; or you can make a "cold call" to a law firm and see what you get.

Interviewing counsel is an opportunity to get a lot of free information.

Through the process of interviewing counsel, you can learn a lot about your issues even as you assess the lawyer. Don't be shy about asking lawyers their opinions about various strategies you may be considering. You can get a lot of information about what is possible to do and how to go about doing it. In some situations, lawyers may be hesitant to express a specific opinion about your matter without having had the opportunity to review the local ordinances and specific facts. If that is the case, you can learn a lot about what facts are important and what sources of information you will need. You can learn how disputes such as yours have played out. Has this lawyer ever worked on one? Ask her. Lawyers also know people in government and in the private sector who may be helpful allies. Follow up on names they suggest. You may speak to many lawyers who you do not subsequently retain, or who may not be able to take on a pro bono case, but they might want to help you in other ways. Frequently that help is in the form of offering information and contacts or being willing to react to things as they come up to give you some guidance. Try to have as long and detailed a conversation as possible with each candidate. Ask as many questions as you can. Some won't be answered. You will be surprised at how many will be.

Cost and other criteria: It never hurts to ask.

Before interviewing legal candidates, think about cost limitations and other specific criteria you have. Whereas cost is certainly a factor, I would recommend that you first try to find the best lawyer you can for the task. Your friend's nephew's brother-in-law's cousin might do it for free, but if she has no relevant experience or only handles collections, it might not be a good fit. Look for expertise in the area, along with enthusiasm for the cause. Some combination of those traits should yield excellent counsel.

It never hurts to ask someone to help you out pro bono—that is, for free. Some people may do this as a matter of conscience. Many law firms commit to a certain amount of pro bono work. Often, however, there are written criteria and a committee that uses a selection process to choose pro bono projects; you may not have the time to wait or may not qualify.

Most likely, you will be billed for legal work. If that's the case, negotiate the rate and expenses. Find out how the billing works. Will you be billed the full rate for travel time and attendance at meetings? Often lawyers will negotiate lower fees for these matters. Are there tasks that could be handled by a paralegal or secretary, such as getting documents or searching courthouse records? Talk about getting the most "bang for the buck." Most lawyers who want to represent you on a land battle will make an effort to accommodate your limited pocketbook. If you have a ceiling on costs, talk about that. Your lawyer needs to know if she has to act tactically. Do you want to be informed when a certain level of costs has been incurred? It is reasonable to ask your lawyer to let you know when she has spent a certain amount. It is fair to monitor closely what is being done and whether you are getting value for your money.

The bottom line, however, is that you get what you pay for. You want someone with expertise and enthusism for the assignment. It can be short-sighted to "nickel and dime" someone to the point that there is no mutual trust in the attorney-client relationship.

As a general matter, I believe it makes sense to hire the best professional you can find, and then let that person get the job done. The process of micromanagement will only cost you more and hinder the process. It is a matter of balance between keeping informed and controlling the process. Let your counsel do the job you are paying her for.

When interviewing counsel, articulate your other needs and requirements. For Fischer Creek, we wanted someone who would work closely and comfortably with me. I was able to do a lot of fact gathering, legal research, and even letter drafting. We wanted someone who would review my work and fill in the gaps as needed, rather than do everything. This was a major way we could keep our bills down and use counsel for specific tasks that only they could perform. For example, for certain letters and meetings, it was critical that our counsel show their full force.

Who will be the contact person? As a matter of efficiency, as well as to keep the bills down, you should designate only one person to be the contact person for counsel. Everyone should funnel questions or suggestions through the contact person. If you have a lawyer on your team who is not going to represent you, that person may be good for this task. Remember: Time is money. Every phone call, every question, costs money. Lawyers only have their time to sell. It is your responsibility to use your lawyer's time wisely.

How counsel affects the dynamics of a development battle

In all three of my development battles, counsel played a crucial—and different—role.

Fischer Creek: Strategic use of counsel

Counsel was important in the fight for Fischer Creek, but our use of it was intermittent and highly strategic. In other words, we pulled counsel in at specific times for specific purposes. There were four main situations in which we deployed counsel to participate actively in the fight.

1. Slowing and controlling the process

Early in the process of fighting the annexation, the Friends of Fischer Creek asked counsel to communicate directly with the Village of Cleveland in person and by letter. We wanted to establish our credibility and seriousness early on and set the rules and tone for future debate. The first plan commission meeting on Fischer Creek was in mid-September, and on October 7 our counsel, William TeWinkle, wrote the village a letter. The village was intending to force a vote on annexation quickly. TeWinkle pointed out the legal deficiencies in holding the vote and indicated we would seek judicial review (that is, sue them) if the vote were held as scheduled. He also requested a settlement conference (which the village never allowed) and urged the village to review the annexation process carefully. Real message: We will be reviewing the annexation process carefully, so you better do it right.

Not long thereafter, one of TeWinkle's associates, Peter Mayer, attended a village board meeting and spoke about various legal requirements and the concerns of his clients. This served several purposes. Most important, we really were concerned with the village's following required procedures. In the strongest way possible, we wanted to tell the village that it needed to follow the law, follow the time periods required by law, perform all the reviews, and hold all the hearings required by law. Like it or not, people often listen more carefully to the message when it is delivered by a lawyer. Mayer's statement of how the village had to proceed according to the law and due process undoubtedly got more attention coming from him than it would have coming from one of us. Hiring a lawyer showed we were serious, intended to stick around, and were a force to be dealt with. In other communities, at another time, hiring a lawyer might not be perceived that way. At that time, in the Village of Cleveland, retaining a lawyer sent a strong message.

2. Responding to the developer's legal attack on the Friends of Fischer Creek
We needed our counsel to respond to threats from the developer's lawyers. After the Friends of Fischer Creek had succeeded in slowing the process and even casting doubt on the inevitability of the annexation, the developer became increasingly concerned and frustrated.

In early November, I was served with a letter from the developer's Chicago counsel, which threatened myself and the Friends of Fischer Creek with a "SLAPP suit" (Strategic Lawsuits Against Public Participation), a device developers were using nationally to silence public opposition to development projects). In the letter, the developers demanded

> . . . that the Friends immediately cease . . . all written and oral communications to any and all parties, whether the county of Manitowoc, the village of Cleveland, the owner of the property, the Wisconsin Department of Natural Resources or any other party.

TeWinkle replied with a wonderful letter on behalf of the Friends. It still qualifies as one of my all-time favorite legal communications. TeWinkle wrote, "I don't know how they do things in Chicago, but in this part of the country citizens still have the right to associate and exercise free speech (reference: The Constitution of the United States.)" What a choice example of how a lawyer can be effective without requiring a lot of research or incurring large expenses!

Whatever the developer thought he was gaining for himself, he didn't. He did accomplish some good things for the Friends, however. The threat fueled our media campaign and won us our first supporting editorial in the *Sheboygan Press,* which praised us for our courage and tenacity. It also gave me an opportunity to address the plan commission. In my remarks, I noted:

> This heavy-handed threat demonstrates how this developer views your fellow citizens of the Village of Cleveland. This Chicago law firm suggests that by becoming involved in the decisions impacting this community, those who live here are doing things that they describe as "actionable," when in fact, what the Friends of Fischer Creek are doing is called democracy.

The developer handed us a goldmine of opportunity. We looked at the board and plan commission and said: How can you trust these people? Do you want to deal with them? Look at how they treat us — do you really know what you're getting into? Do you want to put the future of the village in their hands? Even the village president, Gary Schmitz, an advocate for the development, expressed regret at the developer's action and admitted that this was not going to further the developer's cause.

3. Mounting a referendum campaign

A third strategic use of counsel was the decision to mount a referendum. When the referendum became a tool to implement our strategy, we needed counsel to advise us on the intricate state requirements for procedure and wording. Here, counsel worked behind the scenes, advising us on how to word the petitions, how to circulate them, exactly how to word the referendum, and how to undertake other matters related to the arcane legal process.

4. Challenging board procedural shenanigans

Finally, a different lawyer stepped in to help us pro bono after the election on an issue of village procedure. When the village railroaded a vote for a vacancy on the board by refusing to let a board member change her vote when she had obviously misspoken, the village then supplied an opinion of its counsel justifying the actions. The son-in-law of one of the Friends, who worked at a law firm in Milwaukee, used his own expertise and the resources of his firm to send a detailed opinion letter contrary to the village counsel's. The village counsel backed off, possibly because of the village's fear of getting sued and the likeliness of our success, and the vote was annulled and taken again.

Point Creek: Land negotiations and purchase

For the Point Creek project, our lawyer handled one big piece of the project for us. During the Point Creek battle, we were working two major tracks simultaneously: fund-raising and negotiating with the landowner. After the initial phase of the project, our counsel undertook all dealings with the landowner. There were several reasons for this. The landowner was difficult, and our lawyer was the only person on the team who could handle him. Also, the landowner played people off against each other, so we needed someone who could work alone to handle all communications with him and control information flow. Finally, we needed to negotiate a land contract, various amendments to the land contract, and a complicated five-party escrow closing. Much of that work had to be handled by experienced real estate counsel.

Meanwhile, I had my hands full lining up the $1.9 million financing and then conducting a major lobbying effort to get our DNR funds out of committee in Madison during a period of intensely partisan budget negotiations.

Hika Conservancy: Fighting a zoning change

Developers purchased 550 feet of Lake Michigan frontage adjoining Hika Park in a historic neighborhood of single-family homes. The new owners initially proposed a thirty-six-unit condominium development. In the face of opposition to this proposal, they proposed a townhouse development, although they never disclosed a specific number of units or a site plan.

Opposition came from two fronts. Neighbors attended meetings, wrote letters, and called village officials to protest the development and to advocate purchase of the land as a park. If the decision had been made based on the will of the neighborhood, the zoning change and proposed development would have been defeated. Initially, both the plan commission and the board ignored the public outcry. However, as the developers proved less reliable and opposition held firm, certain board members became more receptive to conservation.

The contiguous neighbors to the north of the land, Otto and Laurel Wimpffen, hired a lawyer to represent their interests. It was the work of their counsel—again, Peter Mayer—that prevented the development from being approved and built that year.

The land-use ordinances of the Village of Cleveland are old and have not been updated to deal with modern land-use issues. In addition, the village has two overlapping and not completely consistent land-use plans in effect. Finally, the zoning category currently in place is a remnant of decades past when the lakeshore was made up of summer cottages and rentals. The zoning category did not contemplate site planning or other typical municipal controls for a modern development. One major issue was whether the proposed townhouses could be built under the current zoning and land-use plans. Did the developer need a zoning change? If so, would any zoning change be consistent with the land-use plans? The law was ambiguous in some of these areas.

It was the Wimpffens' goal to defeat the development or reduce the density as much as possible. Their ultimate goal was for the land to be preserved as a nature conservancy. Another goal was to obtain a "place at the table"; they wanted input on the site planning, drainage, landscaping, lighting, and other matters. They also wanted the developer to come forward with a site plan. All the debates were occurring without any specific proposal from the developer. We wanted to smoke them out.

Amazingly, Peter was able to meet all their goals. This is a success story describing how one couple took a risk, spent some time and money, and defeated a condominium proposal in their back-yard. (Note, however, that community involvement was needed for the second goal, which was convincing the village to purchase the land for a park.) One of the first things that Peter confirmed to the Wimpffens was that, as contiguous neighbors, the ordinances gave them a right of protest. What that meant was that the zoning change had to be approved by three-quarters of the board: Two "no" votes defeated a zoning change. We thought we had those. We did not think the developers knew about these rights until well into the game, and we were not about to tell them.

Peter raised numerous objections to the proposal, starting with procedural deficiencies in the petition. He made many technical points as to why the current zoning does not permit townhouses, and why the land-use plans do not permit a zoning change or a variance allowing townhouses. He also pointed out that the developers' pro-ceeding in the way they were would mean that if they got what they asked for, it would be a nonconforming use and they would not be able to develop it beyond one lot anyway. (I know this is somewhat technical, which is why you need to hire a lawyer!)

In all, the Wimpffens' counsel came up with 12 or 14 problems, any of which would be actionable if the village proceeded with the zoning change. The village board had to pause and consider that if Peter were correct on only one of those points, litigation was likely. He also helped the other neighbors who were objecting to the zon-ing change. In addition to pointing to our other concerns, we could now say, "Shucks, even if this guy is right on only one of his four-teen points, the village seems to be buying a pack of trouble if you approve this."

The most amazing part of Peter's actions, however, was that he managed to ingratiate himself to the village clerk and board all the while. People liked him! The village clerk helped him, and he helped her. They all looked to him for advice. There was no doubt that he would have a place at the table for site planning. His public tack throughout was, "We don't want to stop development. We just want to make sure that it is done in a legal, orderly way. We're here to help."

Legal bills were not low for the Wimpffens. However, they had made a decision that they were committed to the property and to the community and were willing to invest a significant sum to preserve the quiet enjoyment of a place to which they intended to retire. Otto is a teacher; at the time, Laurel ran a program for disabled workers. They are not rich, and the legal fees were not small. It is a choice they made to preserve their property for many years, and it may be a choice you have to make too.

CHAPTER FIVE

BUILD A COALITION AND PARTNERSHIPS
(Strange Bedfellows)

You are going to need community support.

Although one or a few individuals can do a lot, in most development battles you will eventually need community support. Whether your issues are political, requiring support from the electorate, or economic, requiring you to raise large amounts of money, it is likely that your land battle will grow to need and include a variety of people.

For Fischer Creek, the fight was based largely on community values and a message to elected officials concerning the "will of the people." From the start, we knew we needed, and set out to build, grassroots support.

Point Creek was about fund-raising, and we needed community support for that effort as well. We never expected to raise $1.9 million solely from community support, but strong community support is an important factor in winning large grants from government and private foundations. The Wisconsin DNR considers broad-based community support as one factor in deciding which projects to fund; and a major foundation in Manitowoc County, the West Foundation, awarded a two-for-one matching grant, which forced us out into the community for more fund-raising.

Point Creek is also an example of how you never know exactly when you will need community support in a land battle. Although we qualified for a stewardship grant through the merit selection process at the agency level, the size of the grant required approval from the Joint Finance Committee of the Wisconsin state legislature. Our grant was held up by politics in the state capitol, and we needed to mount a major lobbying effort immediately to dislodge the funds before our purchase agreement expired. Our list of donors, along with all our partners, was a ready group we could tap for letters, e-mail, and phone calls to Madison.

For the Hika Conservancy project, community support was also important. The Wimpffens and their lawyer handled one part of that fight with legal arguments to stop the zoning change. However, their legal fight occurred in the wider context of the community. The issue of a zoning change invariably affects a lot of people in the zoning district. Residents of the Hika neighborhood rallied strongly against the zoning change requested by the developers. I do not know if the Wimpffens would have gone to the expense and personal sacrifice of fighting the zoning change without strong community support. They had a ready alternative—sell their land at a tidy profit and move on. But they had their eye on the possibility of turning the land into a nature conservancy. Community support would be required to convince the village to remove the land from the tax rolls, raise the funds to purchase it, and then preserve it permanently as a conservancy park.

Coalitions start to form on their own.

Whether or not you think you need a coalition, it will begin to form on its own. When you personally start to get involved in a cause by attending meetings, writing letters, and gathering information, you encounter like-minded people. Other citizens may also attend a meeting, to speak or to listen. Word will get out that you have an interest. People will call you with questions. This is the start of your coalition, and perhaps even of the leadership circle.

How to build your coalition

It takes work to get all interested parties involved and then to keep their interest and energy focused on the land battle. A good way to start building your coalition is by networking. Make a list of everyone you know who might be sympathetic to the cause. Have others in your nucleus group do the same. If your issue is going to require po-

litical activism, hold an organizational meeting to discuss the issues
and what needs to be done.

Choosing a name

Early in the process of building a coalition, you need a clear idea of
what you stand for and what you are trying to do. You need written
materials to recruit people to your cause. The first step is to come up
with a name. Having a name will also help with media exposure and
will certainly be necessary if you issue a press release.

Some people like the name to be in the form of an acronym. I'm
not a big fan of that myself; usually they sound forced, created more
for the purpose of spelling out a catchy word than for accurately describing the cause. In my view, it is more important that your name
accurately reflects your beliefs and mission than that it sounds clever.
Ultimately, how you define yourself in your name will be an important factor in whether people want to join forces with you or not and
in how you are perceived. Think carefully about meaning and tone
and choose a name that fits who you are.

With Fischer Creek, we happened on "Friends of Fischer Creek"
early on, and the name stuck. The name accurately reflected our goal
to protect the creek and surrounding habitat, and it had a nice allitera-
tive sound. We also liked the positive sound of "friends" and wanted
to be perceived as positive—"for" something, rather than hostile and
"against." Choosing a name is not always that simple. Because of
the history of the Friends of Fischer Creek, and the polarizing effect
the battle had on the community, we are hesitant to use the name
"friends" in any other land issues up here. It was more difficult finding a name for our collective efforts on behalf of Hika Conservancy,
and we never did name ourselves.

For Point Creek, we called ourselves the Point Creek Watershed Initiative. Our main purpose was looking for big bucks, so we wanted
something formal and substantial, the kind of name people would
be comfortable writing large checks to. The formal fund-raising was
done through the vehicle of the local land trust, and for tax reasons,
checks had to be written in their name—the Sheboygan Area Land
Conservancy (SALC). That name hurt us more than it helped. SALC
had been formed by Sheboygan residents but served a four-county

area. The Sheboygan founders never considered how insulting the name was to the residents of the other three counties, who were not receptive to being labeled "Sheboygan Area." That's an example of how an acronym might have seemed clever at the time, but hurt the organization in the long run. Point Creek was in Manitowoc County, near the city of Manitowoc. Going to Manitowoc people for funds and support and then having to ask them to make their checks out to "Sheboygan Area" anything hurt us. As we worked on building support for the Point Creek Watershed Initiative in Manitowoc County, we found that at the start of every meeting or conversation we had to explain that SALC served four counties and that we would change the name. Not the best start to a fund-raising meeting. We had a sub-program of SALC, called the Fischer Creek Alliance, to work in Southeast Manitowoc County. That confused people even more, because we were fund-raising for Point Creek, not for Fischer Creek. Also, because of the political acrimony generated in the fight for Fischer Creek, we did not want to be directly associated with that bit of history in our current fund-raising efforts. Name changes all around were put on the agenda, but the organization's board, which was not active in the trenches, never saw it as a priority.

As soon as you have a name, you become a force. In general, your opponents will try to marginalize you. For example, during Fischer Creek, we were called a "minority of dissidents" (until we won the next election, that is). As soon as you have a name, you are elevated from being a couple of disgruntled people raising objections at a meeting to being one of the "players," along with local government and the developer. It is amazing how much power and credibility a name gives you. It represents organization and support, sometimes well beyond what you actually have. Should you need publicity, it is a big boost to your media efforts. Now the newspapers have someone they can quote in addition to the developer and government officials. It adds conflict and drama to the story and makes for better reporting.

If you are anticipating a big campaign, you may want to design a logo. We did that for Fischer Creek, partly because it happened to be convenient. I doubt we would have researched graphic designers and hired one on our own, but Rolf had a friend who does graphic design. She created a round logo that said "Friends of Fischer Creek" and depicted a great blue heron in flight. We used the logo a lot—on press releases, letterhead, T-shirts, baseball caps, and audio-video presentations. This is another example of how you can use the talents of people within your coalition to forward your cause.

Producing written materials

Whether or not you have a name or a logo, you will need to get the word out about what is happening. For Fischer Creek, we prepared a one-page form specifically for the purpose of recruiting support. It was very simple. It had the logo at the top and stated:

> Friends of Fischer Creek is a community-based organization with the following mission:
> To encourage a long-range plan for growth in the Village of Cleveland and Town of Centerville which is in harmony with nature and consistent with the values of our community.

We had a tear-off return form for people to send in, with or without a donation.

We tried to communicate a lot in that short mission statement. We emphasized "community-based," because the developer was from out of town and one issue was people from outside the community controlling our destiny. We emphasized planning, because we believed that major changes like those proposed by the developer and the village should be planned and debated before being implemented. Also, planning takes time and that fed into our strategy of delay. We talked about growth to make it clear that we were not "antigrowth," something the village officials and developers alleged. We emphasized nature because we value it, and we talked about community values—the "apple-pie-and-mom" approach. It is hard for people to oppose community values. We wanted to portray ourselves as the voice of the community and to lump the village government in with the developer, which was pretty much true.

For Point Creek, our approach was quite different. Because we were soliciting major donations, we put together a fancy spiral-bound booklet of information and color photographs. For grassroots support and smaller donations, we prepared a one-page fact sheet with photographs, along with a request for donations, based upon the materials in the booklet. Because Point Creek is a major stopover for great blue herons—dozens at a time have been photographed at the mouth of the creek—we used one of those pictures as an identifier on all our Point Creek materials. That picture became in effect our "logo" for the campaign. It was an effective visual that spoke "a thousand words" about what we were trying to preserve and why.

For Hika Conservancy, we prepared a one-page fact sheet that explained the issues before the plan commission and board and what was being proposed for the community, and distributed it door to door in the Hika neighborhood. At this point we had a small organization and no name, and a few people squawked about the "anonymous" leaflet. To the best of our knowledge, however, most people appreciated receiving the information. Without a local newspaper or timely village newsletter in Cleveland, it is often difficult for citizens to find out what is going on. Getting the word out is especially important and appreciated here. As small towns lose their local newspapers, dissemination of information becomes more important and more challenging. As a general matter, it is better to have members of your group put their names on any written materials that you distribute. To the extent that these are respected members of the community, the names add credibility to your discussion. Clearly attributed local authorship anchors your cause in the community and discourages allegations that you are "outside agitators."

Distributing your materials

Once your materials are ready, you have to distribute them. You can use various methods, alone or in combination. Each of the people in your nucleus group can send the materials to everyone they know who might be interested. For Fischer Creek, that's how we got most of our initial members and support. For Point Creek, it was an important way to get support and smaller donations. Another effective means is door-to-door distribution. During Fischer Creek, we did a number of door-to-door distributions of various materials to gain support, convey information, and campaign for the election and referendum. Mostly we just did it ourselves and enlisted children to help. Sometimes formal groups like the Boy Scouts or Girl Scouts will help. Another way of delivering materials is to seek the help of another group that is doing a mass distribution in your area. In Cleveland, the Boy Scouts delivered the village newsletter door-to-door. They agreed to distribute leaflets for the Friends of Fischer Creek at the same time. That actually caused a ruckus (everything we did caused a ruckus), and it led to a change in policy prohibiting such subversive activities as distribution of "non-official" materials. But it got our materials out to every home in the village at an important time. If you are fund-raising, you may have more avenues for distribution than if you are pursuing something that is politically controversial.

How to use your supporters

Typically, you want to build a coalition for its electoral power so that you can marshal support when and where you need it. Support may take the form of attendance at meetings, letter writing, telephone calls to commission and board members, donations to cover expenses and counsel, fund-raising activities, envelope stuffing and distribution, circulating petitions, and other organizational help. Make a note of what each member's expertise is.

For Fischer Creek, one of our supporters worked at the local bank, and she helped set up a checking account, got us checks at no cost, and helped process donations made directly to the bank. Another supporter owned a printing company and did all our printing at cost for materials such as flyers, posters, yard signs, and campaign literature. Another couple had a small computer business in town. They computerized our mailing list, sent faxes, and made photocopies. One supporter was a local historian who provided information on the historical importance of the site. Still another was a science teacher and landscape architect. He provided insight into the ecological diversity of the site and the consequences of development. One of our members was a quiet grandmother, but she was great at taking petitions door-to-door. Another supporter was a semiretired lawyer in the town who hung back during the political battles in the village but supplied crucial contacts with the governor's office when our funding request got to that level.

As you get recruits, ask them to continue the recruiting process within their circle of acquaintances. Pretty soon you will have a lot of your community covered and will also have support from people living elsewhere. All this support is beneficial, but be careful about how you characterize your support. Money and donations help no matter where they come from. It is good to use the "think globally; act locally" approach. But on purely local, electoral matters, make sure constituents are taking the lead. Keep good records. It will help you time and again if you have a spreadsheet with your supporters' addresses and telephone numbers in a format that allows you to print address labels for mailings easily. This will save you lots of time and headaches down the road.

Politics makes strange bedfellows.

You may be surprised at who will (and won't!) support you. Through my work on various conservation matters, I became friendly with many people I would not have otherwise met. Sometimes we got support from people I would have initially thought unlikely to get involved. Some people will not want to commit at first. That's okay. They may come to a meeting to learn more about what is going on. Even if they stand at the back and remain quiet, it's good. Government officials know that people aren't there to support "business as usual." Local government knows the issue is important enough to draw people to the meetings and knows it is being watched. That in itself can temper behavior and decision making.

Some people shy away from controversy or from taking a stand that might offend their family, friends, or neighbors. Sometimes these people will help from behind the scenes in ways that still protect their privacy. Use what they offer and include them. They may have skills, like computer literacy, that are valuable. Sometimes they can give important insights into the thinking of the community or government officials. My own approach tends to be up front: I take a stand and let people know what it is. That's good, in that I get fired up and get stuff done. But it's not always good if you are looking to include people on the fence, because it can scare people off. A good leadership circle includes people of different styles and temperaments. This allows you to reach the most people. Put together a group of people with a variety of skills, and let people do what they do best. Usually, that's what they want to do and what they enjoy doing. It's the obvious way to enlist help.

Hold your own meetings.

You may want to hold your own meetings. In some circumstances, local government and local press provide an adequate platform to make your views known. In other circumstances, there is active repression of free debate or simply a lack of opportunity for an open discussion. During the fight for Fischer Creek, we sponsored several public meetings. We advertised the meetings and invited the public and the press. We saw a number of advantages to holding our own meetings:

1. We showed the breadth of our support, or at least the number of people interested in our point of view and concerned about the course of events.
2. We put forth our concerns and opinions without the limitations of time and style set by the village. Typically our only chance to speak was during the short "public input session" at the beginning of each meeting. We were limited in time and limited in topic to the agenda set for that meeting. We did not have the opportunity to react to what occurred during the meeting.
3. We presented our vision. Instead of appearing negative and critical as we might at village meetings, in which we had to react to the agenda and actions of the government, we could present our own positive vision for the community and our view of the appropriate process for making development decisions.
4. We took control of the debate. Instead of always having to react to the village's and developer's agenda, we set our own agenda. They now had to react to us.
5. We showcased our leaders. This lent further credibility to our actions throughout the battle.
6. We rallied more support. Some people who had not attended village meetings or contacted us previously came to the community-wide meeting.
7. It was a way to communicate with village, town, and county offi-

cials in a neutral setting. Some village officials wanted to know more about what we were thinking and what we had learned. These meetings provided a less adversarial forum for them to get a great deal more information than they were getting in politically charged official meetings.

Other methods of building support

We used other methods to build support and momentum as well. We printed bright green signs with the Friends of Fischer Creek logo and "Save Fischer Creek" and asked people to put a sign in their window. It was a passive but highly visible method of showing support. To see support, all you had to do was drive around the village. It kept the issue constantly on the front burner, which is hard to do.

We sold T-shirts with the Friends of Fischer Creek logo. We made buttons, but those never became popular. We tried an acronym, PERC (Public Environmental Resource Center), which I thought was pretty clever at the time, but it never took off. We had fund-raising parties. One supporter was a musician and wrote a song. We also held a silent auction for a watercolor study of Fischer Creek by a prominent local artist, Robert Heuel, who also allowed us to photograph one of his oil paintings of Fischer Creek (one of our supporters was a professional photographer). From the photo we made high-quality prints for sale. This was great fund-raising, as well as an effective means of furthering the support for and visibility of our cause. The *Sheboygan Press* ran a front-page article with color photographs about the painting and our reproductions. It gave us great publicity at a time when we were not in the news for other reasons.

How to forge partnerships

In addition to building support among individuals, you also want to forge partnerships with other organizations. This is important for many reasons. Your cause is like a snowball rolling downhill. It is hard to get it going at first, but it gets bigger and goes faster as it gains momentum. Organizational support is a great way to get that snowball moving.

Other organizations can be enlisted as supporters, partners, or members of your coalition. I like the term "partner" because it elevates organizational support, setting it apart from individual support. Also, "partner" has become somewhat of a buzzword for identifying the breadth of your support. Whatever you call it, organizational support builds credibility and makes it easier to muster additional organizational and individual support. Getting organizational support can be an efficient way of getting individual support as well, because all those organizations have members who might be rallied to your cause.

If you are applying for grant money, you may be asked to list supporting organizations. Sometimes you get extra points based on partnerships or alliances with other organizations.

It is likely that some organizational support may come from groups that are not strictly within the local unit of government that is the site of the land battle. You have to assess your own situation, but my experience has been that, generally, organizational support helps no matter where it originates. Many conservation issues have regional effects far beyond the local unit of government charged with the par-ticular decision at issue. Bringing in the larger world may help focus minds on the global impact. Even if a supporting organization is not part of the voting constituency, local government may pause as an issue becomes regional and people from the outside are seen to be looking at what is happening. Partnerships can also serve to educate local politicians on the importance and regional effect of an issue.

Getting started with local groups

There are probably some local organizations that you can count on for early support. People in a community can usually identify these ready and faithful organizations. Someone in your leadership group probably has connections with conservation and environmental groups in your area. Some of your supporters will belong to other organizations that might lend support. In our area, we have an active Sheboygan Sierra Club chapter that supports conservation initiatives throughout the community. They can be counted on for writing letters of support and letters to the editor on many conservation causes. Ask your supporters for names of organizations to contact. Often, your supporters will be happy to make contact with their groups. Some organizations avoid political controversy but will support a pure conservation effort. Others will take a stand even if politics is involved. We have successfully approached local garden clubs and hunting and fishing groups. It would not hurt to ask local service organizations, such as the Lions, the Kiwanis, athletic clubs, and the Rotary Club. Even organizations that cannot support you may let you speak to their group. This can garner organizational support or additional individual supporters.

Know what you want before you ask.

Know what you want from these organizations. Are you asking for a letter of support? Is the letter to support a grant application, or is it for a political cause? Sometimes you don't need anything in writing, but you just want to use the organization's name in a list of supporters that will be distributed in a grants application or to the media. Rolf Johnson compiled a list of support for Point Creek with the name of the organization and the individual's name in parentheses. That was a clever bit of packaging, because it appeared that we had extensive institutional support, when in fact we had extensive support from individuals affiliated with various institutions.

If other organizations support you, tell the organizations that you are approaching. There is a bandwagon effect. Do you want them to send you a letter of support on their letterhead? Do you want them to write a local politician? Do you want them to write a letter to the editor or write a guest editorial? Do you want to ask their members to write letters or make calls? Do you want a financial contribution? Do you want to use any of their resources? Be specific. Be realistic in your requests.

Conservation organizations

An obvious place to look for partners is in other conservation organizations. Think broadly, and go after groups at the regional and state level. Are you trying to save a river or watershed? Talk to other watershed environmental groups in your state. Are you saving farmland? There are a lot of organizations active in preserving farmland that may be able to help you. Our issues involved the Lake Michigan Watershed, so we looked for support from the Lake Michigan Federation, Great Lakes United, and other Great Lakes research and conservation groups, as well as river and watershed organizations. The Nature Conservancy (TNC) may support or lend its name, even if the land in question does not meet TNC's standards for its own project. Some organizations, like the Audubon Society, may have local chapters. There are undoubtedly many other conservation organizations based in towns in your state or in your state capital.

In Wisconsin, regional hunting organizations are strong allies of conservation efforts because we are preserving the habitat needed to support bird and animal populations. Your supporters may belong to local fish and game chapters, Trout Unlimited, or Ducks Unlimited. If not, contact these groups yourself. These alliances may fall into the category of "politics makes strange bedfellows" if you are queasy about allies who promote hunting. But, around here, hunting organizations have a lot of political sway and large memberships. Politicians are wary of offending the hunters, but they might not care as much about environmentalists.

Are there any environmental centers in your area? Often the director will support conservation efforts in the community. We received support from the Maywood Environmental Center in Sheboygan and from Woodland Dunes in Manitowoc County. Members of local environmental centers are also good candidates to support your cause. Ask for a list of members or donors. Often, newsletters for these organizations will list them. I have found that, generally, these organizations will share names to support a cause with which they are sympathetic. Directors at these centers are also good sources of information, able to advise you on everything from the ecology of your geographical area to the politics of land acquisition.

Support from government entities

You may be able to gather support from individuals in a variety of government units and agencies. We got support from the DNR and from Manitowoc County on several big initiatives. Sometimes, one of these officials can attend local meetings. The director of Manitowoc County Parks and Planning, Jerry Kirchener, attended the first public meeting given by the Friends and spoke about the county's long interest in acquiring Fischer Creek.

County officials can provide a county-wide view of what is going on and discuss the county's potential role in land issues. County employees know the county's land-use standards, pending regulations concerning land use, and the land-use trends in the county. County standards may be different from local standards. Even if the county standards do not apply as a matter of law, just knowing that different standards exist can help make local officials consider the wisdom of their decisions. Support from the county (as well as from other government units) can help sympathetic local officials stay the course. Sometimes local officials do not want to be sitting alone on an issue; support from other government units helps them.

For Fischer Creek, we had the strong support of the Town of Centerville's chairman, largely because the developer wanted to annex land from the town to the village. We also had support from many town residents who had a strong conservation ethic. Interestingly, the same town chairman opposed the conservation of Point Creek because he did not want to lose the tax base.

Because Point Creek mainly involved purchase of the land directly from the landowner and did not require any town action, we succeeded despite this opposition. It was therefore important that we had strong grassroots support county-wide, including from many residents of the town. That was one example of a situation in which we did not think we needed grassroots support at first, but it proved to be critically important to our ultimate success.

Support from colleges and universities

Another source of partners is colleges and universities. Whereas local officials may or may not be swayed by academic support, academics are critical in building credibility, garnering media attention, and building momentum for your cause. Universities have a lot of information and can help as you are researching and identifying the issues. Universities have experts on such topics as biodiversity, conservation biology, planning, and law who are often willing to help you.

The academic community was important in both Fischer Creek and Point Creek. For Fischer Creek, we made contact with a professor in urban planning at the University of Wisconsin in Madison, Dr. Jack Huddleston, who was an expert on urban sprawl and the economics of development. He provided extensive information on what Cleveland faced with a development of such magnitude and confirmed my instinct that the development would affect the village in countless ways that village officials had never considered. Dr. Huddleston came to Cleveland to meet with plan commission and board members. He discussed the process of "visioning" in making decisions that materially affect the future, the role of planning in such decisions, and the many consequences of development on a village. Jack was invaluable to me as I researched issues on development and needed guidance on how to react to the assumptions and statements of the developer and local politicians.

Three universities became full-fledged partners in the Point Creek Watershed Initiative. Initially, our entire attention was on how to raise almost two million dollars to purchase the land. As we began to accumulate the funding, we had to face a whole new set of issues, namely, who would own the land and who would manage the land. Federal grant requirements were clear that the land had to be owned by a LUG (local unit of government). We convinced the county to be our LUG, but they made it clear that they would hold the deed and not commit to active management that could involve expenditure of resources. That left open the issue of who would manage the land.

We put together a consortium of three institutions that agreed to manage the property if we succeeded in the purchase: University of Wisconsin, Sheboygan; University of Wisconsin, Manitowoc; and University of Wisconsin, Green Bay. University support helped in numerous ways, in addition to its important function as property manager. Having the universities as partners helped immeasurably with our fund-raising from both public and private sources. The government-granting agencies wanted to see permanent, responsible parties in charge of managing the property. Even if the Sheboygan Area Land Conservancy had agreed to perform this function, it was too small and too new to satisfy the granting agencies. Also, having three universities involved gave us superb scientific and educational credentials, which helped us attract private donations and make our case to state legislators during our intense lobbying efforts. In terms of involvement, we were blessed with having the two deans from Manitowoc and Sheboygan personally involved and with having the head of the Cofrin Center for Biodiversity act as our contact at University of Wisconsin, Green Bay (UWGB). We had three eminent people, as well as the institutions behind them, actively supporting our efforts. University involvement was also a new angle to offer the media and helped us get additional coverage on a stale story. After the partnerships were in place, articles featuring the colleges and deans appeared on the front pages of the Manitowoc and Sheboygan newspapers.

Finally—and this point often gets lost in the shuffle as you try to get something done—having university partners manage Point Creek was the right solution, not just an expedient one. UWGB was already managing land in conservation directly south of the Point Creek property. The involvement of UWGB was going to enable all the land to be managed under one set of guiding principles, which makes sense for one contiguous area of land. It also enabled coordinated research to be conducted.

Tapping into the land-trust community

Your local and state land trusts are another source of partners. The Point Creek project was done under the auspices of the local land trust. As discussed in detail in Chapter Eight, if you are doing significant fund-raising, you will need to channel funds through either a public entity or a "501(c)(3)" tax-exempt organization. Your local land trust could be an obvious choice. Land trusts cannot lobby extensively, because of their tax-exempt status, so their active support will be for projects that do not have a highly political component. Even for politically sensitive projects, your local land trust may be willing to write letters in support of your project. It may even be able to donate money towards purchase of the land, or help in raising money. Land trusts can also supply information about conservation easements, which may be a useful tool as you are structuring how to preserve land permanently. Land trusts can also communicate with their members to get individual support in the form of donations, lobbying from individuals, letters, or otherwise. Finally, the local land trust leaders are probably knowledgeable in many aspects of conservation and land preservation in your area. They may also know the names of other environmental groups in your region who could offer support.

Business support

Business support may be crucial. More and more, governments are looking for "public-private partnership" as a condition of support. Businesses can help in a number of ways. Cash donations are possible, although we did not have much success in that regard. Many local businesses do give money to local causes, so it is worth a shot. Often they already have their pet projects, whether it is the YMCA, Big Brothers Big Sisters, the local museum, or whatever. Businesses may also be willing to contribute "in kind," whether it is to print materials, provide food for a fund-raiser, permit use of copy machines, or satisfy some other need. Businesses tend to shy away from political controversy but may be able to support an apolitical conservation effort.

Success breeds success.

As you build your grassroots coalition and find partners, you will find that success breeds success. Once you get some organizations to support you, they will put you in touch with other groups that will also be your partners. While the task may seem daunting at first, soon you will have a long list of supporters whose names and resources you can use as needed.

CHAPTER SIX

INFLUENCE LOCAL GOVERNMENT

(Meetings, Meetings, Meetings)

Who is your local government?

The answer to that will vary, depending on where you live and what issues you are addressing. It might be city, village, town, or county— or some combination of these bodies. You need to identify and influence the governmental body that has decision-making authority for the issue at hand. Your battle may involve zoning change, variance, conditional use, site review plans, plat review, building permits, purchasing authority for parks and open space, or land-use planning. One or more bodies, such as the plan commission or the village board, may be responsible for these issues within a government unit; and there may even be more than one governmental unit responsible for different aspects of your land battle.

Once you identify which governmental unit is responsible, you must then figure out which bodies within that governmental unit have responsibility for a particular issue. In the Village of Cleveland, for example, the village has authority for its own zoning changes. An application for zoning change goes first to the plan commission, which either makes a recommendation for the zoning change or declines. Upon recommendation by the plan commission, the application then goes to the village board for approval. Therefore, citizens have two opportunities to defeat a zoning change—at the plan commission and at the board levels. In Cleveland, however, the plan commission has sole authority for review and approval of site plans for subdivisions. In the Town of Centerville, the county approves variances on zoning, but the town issues its own building permits. For annexations to the Village of Cleveland, the plan commission of the village makes a recommendation to the village board, which must pass an annexation by a two-thirds affirmative vote; also, the State of Wisconsin must issue an advisory letter as to whether the annexation is in the public interest.

Land-use procedures are frequently complicated and arcane. Do not assume you know who is responsible for a given approval, the proper procedure, or the time frames required by statute. Determining which statutes the governing body must apply can also be complicated. For example, in the Village of Cleveland, lakeshore land is governed by two different statutory authorities. For land in the village, village rules generally apply. However, for land annexed into the village after a certain date, county rules apply. What this means is that two houses next to each other on the Lake Michigan bluff may be subject to two different statutory setbacks. (For all towns in Manitowoc County, there is overlapping jurisdiction between the town and the county for shore land within one thousand feet of Lake Michigan. That means a landowner must comply with both statutory schemes.)

Do not assume that your local government knows the proper law or procedure. At least at the village level, my experience has been that they often get it wrong. There have been a number of occasions during a ten-year period when lawyers hired by citizens have educated the village as to its own ordinances. At the county level, however, my experience has been that there is generally a good understanding of applicable statutes and regulations. In fact, we often relied on advice from the county as we researched the ordinances applicable to a given situation. However, I have also seen decisions that were clearly wrong in terms of prevailing law and were subject to challenge.

Meetings, meetings, meetings

Why aren't you serving on the school board, village board, or church council? For me, and a lot of people I know, it's because we hate meetings. As you pursue the goal of getting favorable government action on a land-use issue, you may find yourself attending more (expletive deleted!) meetings than you ever imagined in your worst nightmare.

Democratic government does things by open meeting. It is the backbone and the curse of democracy. It is critically important that you attend all these meetings, and get other people to attend them also. You have to keep the pressure on, speak out on your issues if given the opportunity and let the decision makers know that they are being watched. My experience is that the mere presence of concerned citizens (and the press) may temper extreme behavior.

As others join your effort, you will start having your own meetings to strategize about what to do concerning the board and plan commission meetings and public works and county meetings that you have been attending. If you are particularly frustrated with the agenda and conduct of the governments' meetings, you may decide to call your own public meetings for concerned citizens, at which you set the agenda and provide your coalition the opportunity to speak. Meetings beget meetings.

For some people, getting involved in local issues proves a natural transition into government service. When you are sitting through meetings, listening to other people miss the point and misrepresent the point, there may come a time when you decide it would be easier to serve on the board or commission. You figure, "I'm going to all these meetings anyway, and it will be less frustrating and more effective to participate in the discussions and vote." This is generally a good transition—for the cause, if not for your mental health—because part of the natural progression of a land battle is to change the people serving in office if you can't change their minds. More on that below.

Scenario One: The cooperative LUG

All government bodies are different; all land battles are different. The dynamic of your land battle, mind-set of the public servants, sophistication and personality of your coalition, and the historical context all contribute to your decisions about how to proceed. As a general matter, however, despite these differences, there are identifiable patterns on how land battles evolve.

In some land battles, the battle is with the developer. In other words, the battle is against time to raise money for a land purchase and to beat out a developer for control of the property. In this scenario, the local unit of government (LUG) is not directly involved in your battle. If the LUG wants the development, government may not affirmatively help your efforts. If the LUG has the money to purchase the land for conservation, you probably do not have a land battle. In other cases, the burden is on you to control the property, but the LUG could be more in the nature of your partner. Even if you commence your organization and fund-raising with the notion that you are acting totally independently of government, you may find that you do need government down the road.

This is what happened with our Point Creek project. We began raising money through a tax-exempt land conservancy and thought we could retain control of the project. However, we soon realized we would need money from public sources as well as from private foundations and individuals. When we investigated particular public grants, we learned that grants could only be applied for and awarded to a LUG, not to a private not-for-profit organization such as a land conservancy. At that point, we approached Manitowoc County to see if it would apply for the grants (if we continued to do all the work) and then hold the deed on the property if we were successful in completing a purchase.

We were extremely fortunate to have the full cooperation of Manitowoc County. However, that cooperation came, in part, because we also understood their needs and proceeded by their rules.

Luckily, the director of parks and planning, Mike Demske, had a sophisticated understanding of the value of open space and realized that open space can benefit a community economically by encouraging future development near but not on the environmental resource. Centerville was historically a town of dairy farmers. The land values of many dairy farmers centered around preservation of farmland. Other land, such as lake frontage and woodlots, was thought of as expendable. More modern land values emphasize the importance of preserving the precious limited resource of Lake Michigan shoreline, wildlife habitat, public access to undeveloped land, and the enhanced property values of the surrounding town and county. Given the shrinking number of family farmers in Centerville, the amount of other land available for development there, and the high value most people place on lake frontage, Demske and the Manitowoc County Parks Commission would not allow the town chairman to derail the purchase.

We cooperated as well. Demske proposed that any money raised from logging the pinewoods at Point Creek be shared with the town to compensate them for lost tax revenue on the parcel. Even in its current undeveloped state, the Point Creek property generated some tax revenue for the town, which would be lost when the land moved to county ownership. We agreed in principle, but the issue will be revisited if and when logging occurs.

It helped that we knew exactly what we needed from the county. Initially, we only required its signature as the sponsoring LUG on our Wisconsin Coastal Management Program grant application. Recognizing its limited resources, we were highly selective in asking the county for help. Accordingly, it stepped up to the plate whenever we did ask. For example, for the application we needed the county's computerized mapping capabilities to show the location of the site and the plat numbers. Later on, when Wisconsin Coastal Management Program withheld approval of our grant pending a proposal for public access, the county immediately mapped a proposed trail system. The county did have some state-funded resources, in the form of the Wisconsin Conservation Corps, for building a parking lot and clearing trails. We accommodated the county in terms of being ready to work when the volunteer conservation corps had time for Point Creek. Finally, we held our breath awaiting approval from the planning and parks commission and from the full county board for our grant applications. Frankly, we were plain lucky that the parks commission and county board did not have any political problems related to the purchase. Different timing could have produced a different outcome.

Scenario Two: The adversarial LUG

In some situations, government does not have an entrenched viewpoint regarding development. In that fortunate scenario, citizens can educate local government and apply pressure to get the LUG to vote for a conservation solution. In other situations, the LUG is prejudiced in favor of development and is clearly adversarial to citizens' proposing alternatives to development.

In the case of Hika Conservancy, the majority of board members initially favored the developer but began to change their minds as new information about the limitations for development on the site and citizens' feelings in favor of a conservancy came out. The board, under President Cindy Huhn, followed mandated procedures, gave citizens time to express their views, and maintained institutional neutrality during the process. Here, citizen activism really did change the outcome.

For Fischer Creek, the entrenched leadership of the plan commission and board was openly hostile to the citizens and favorable to the developer. That leadership was ready to ignore procedure and citizen input in order to annex the land and approve the development. That outcome would have been realized but for the relentless campaign by the Friends of Fischer Creek, actions by our legal counsel, and extensive press coverage.

In both situations, however, we and other citizens endeavored to "take the high road" and present ourselves as positive and cooperative. We tried to unite and find common ground with our opponents. For Fischer Creek, this became increasingly difficult because, in fact, the community was split into factions. Nonetheless, our communications were positive. We made statements as to what we value in the community, discussed the need for balance, and eventually presented our own vision and community plan. However, we did not hesitate to contradict the developer's false, incomplete, and inaccurate information every step of the way.

For the Hika Conservancy land battle, we used legal counsel to defeat the developer's plans and used public advocacy for a park to bring the board to consider the importance of open space and neighborhood values. In the case of Hika, I do not believe pure advocacy on the part of the residents of the Hika neighborhood would have convinced a majority of the plan commission or board to reject the zoning changes. The legal challenges, which lowered the density from condominiums to single-family homes, served to remove the board's economic assumptions for the project. Once it became clear that tax revenues would be nowhere near what the developer projected, the board was more open to alternatives for the site, including conservancy.

First, try reason.

Some local board and plan commission members are deeply prejudiced in favor of development. Others may have an opinion but remain open to changing their minds. No matter what the perceived mind-set of the LUG, our first course of action was always to discuss the facts. Present your case and provide rational reasons for implementing your recommendations.

During Fischer Creek, we bombarded the plan commission, village board, and citizenry with factual reasons to question, then to reject, the development. We discussed the appropriate process for making such a decision and questioned the wisdom of annexing the land. The following is a summary of some of the information we presented.

Memo on how to proceed

In a written memo, we encouraged the board to:

1. Accept outside help from experts.
2. Accept help from citizens.
3. Not rely on answers from the developer.
4. Treat the situation as an arm's-length business negotiation with the developer.
5. Remember that the key card in the negotiation is the annexation—once the village annexes, it loses its negotiating power.
6. Take time to understand the issues and formulate a position.
7. Not let the developer divide and conquer the village.
8. Actively set the agenda, rather than letting the developer formulate the debate.

What don't we know?

We prepared a list of unanswered questions (more than seventy-five) about the development. Our questions fell into the following categories:

1. How will the proposed development affect our tax base?
2. How will the proposed development affect the cost of the new wastewater-treatment plant?

3. What has been the experience of other communities that have allowed similar developments?
4. What will be the effect of the increased traffic from the development?
5. What is the environmental impact of the proposed development?
6. What is the historical significance of the area?
7. What are all the short-term and long-term costs to the village?
8. Will the development bring any other economic benefits to the village?

Developer's agreement

We emphasized the point (which most of the board never acknowledged) that the village should enter into a developer's agreement with the developer. In exchange for the village's annexing the land for the development, the developer would make certain legal undertakings to the village as to impact costs, future liabilities, and other matters. We suggested negotiating matters such as:

1. Street maintenance
2. Value of the excess capacity of the new wastewater plant
3. Installation of a new well and pumping station to serve the development
4. Compensation for the increase in taxable value of the community, which would permanently reduce the state revenue-share payment to Cleveland
5. Cost of additional police and fire protection
6. Independent historical and wildlife study of the property, to determine setbacks and other design features of the development, as well as to ensure public access to the lakeshore
7. Bonding and other security for the village until the developer completed sale of the entire development

The board never understood the concept of negotiating leverage and was willing to vote on the annexation without extracting a single concession from the developer. This is a common problem. Small, unsophisticated local governments are being forced to handle matters of great complexity. Often, they are in far over their heads in terms of understanding the decisions they are making and the consequences of their actions. At that time, there were few persons on a board of seven who had the education and business experience to understand how to negotiate a contract that allocated risk and responsibility for a major development.

Development in the balance

We prepared a statement describing the present balance of our community and how this development would upset the balance. We discussed factors such as the balance among:

1. Town and village
2. Dense development and farm, woods, and meadows
3. Developed land, natural land, and waters
4. Varied income levels and occupations
5. Humans and wildlife
6. Tax burdens and the appropriate level of services

We then raised various questions about how the development would affect the balances that the community valued. This questioning led to:

Written comments on developer's preliminary plat. One of the plan commission members opposing the annexation prepared a written response to the developer's preliminary plat, questioning the plat and pointing out deficiencies in the layout and its suitability for the site.

Written responses to each of the developer's statements concerning the issues we raised. We showed in writing that the developer was incorrect or incomplete in his statements to the village about matters such as the projected ongoing costs of the development, the effect of the development on our tax base, the effect on the village's revenue share from the state, the ecological significance of the site, the amount of property taxes generated, and numerous other matters.

Calculation of the net cost of the development. Using a computer model distributed by the Urban Land Institute, we ran a complicated analysis of projected revenues versus projected costs and showed that the development, in the long term, would cost the village more than it generated in revenues. The best-case scenario

was that the development would be a wash in terms of tax benefits. With no tax benefits resulting from the development, then the
social and environmental costs of the development would be seen
as the decisive issue.

Friends of Fischer Creek community vision

We wrote and circulated an extensive community vision and land-
use plan, presenting our positive vision for the land, the village, and
the role of development. We emphasized that Cleveland already had
large amounts of vacant land within current village borders and that
this land should be developed for the long-term health of the village,
whereas sprawl into the countryside should be avoided. The vision
included:

1. A description of the Friends of Fischer Creek
2. The recommendation that the land be a conservation area
3. A section identifying the basis for our quality of life
4. Recommendations on how to grow and maintain the quality of
   life
5. A description of the proposed development—using only the developer's *own words* from his written submissions and statements to the press
6. An economic analysis of the development
7. Expert opinions on how development does not pay for itself
8. The Urban Land Institute computer analysis of the costs of development, in spreadsheet form
9. An analysis of the new wastewater plant and the value of that excess capacity
10. Further analysis of such issues as infrastructure, land planning,
    and social and environmental factors

In the plan, we cited numerous outside authorities for the proposition
that, almost invariably, expenses rise to meet or exceed increased
revenue from development.

We took every opportunity to present rational arguments opposing
annexation. We spoke at every public meeting; we called and met
with village officials; we held our own public meetings, at which we
controlled the agenda; and we met with reporters and issued press

releases. Bit by bit we provided a few courageous board members the ammunition for dissent; bit by bit we convinced the voters that the village government was not acting responsibly in hastily promoting this development.

Use outside experts.

The tactical use of outside experts can add credibility to your fight. Experts can bring regional issues to a local fight. They can also give credibility to your own position. The fact is that officials will often believe something coming from an expert when they discount it coming from their own voters. (Any employee who has watched management rely on outside consultants has seen this!) However, you have to assess your own political situation. It is possible that outsiders could be perceived as a threat or could otherwise harm your cause.

When Jack Huddleston came to Cleveland, the draw of an outside expert enabled us to reach certain people who would not have spent an evening with just the Friends of Fischer Creek. Jack made the following points in his presentation:

1. He takes no position for or against a development proposal; he just lists the points for consideration.
2. The village needs a vision of what its citizens want it to be, before considering any specific development proposals.
3. The most common thing he hears is, "Why, with all this growth, didn't my taxes go down?"
4. The Wisconsin revenue-share calculation means that for every dollar the village collects, it receives only 60 cents in actual tax revenues.
5. The village should place an economic value on the excess capacity of its wastewater plant as a limited resource.
6. The village can negotiate a developer's agreement, but this has to be done before the annexation.
7. Cleveland has five hundred households and this development would add about two hundred homes. This is a *radical* change to the fabric of the village.
8. Property values will go up. Is this an advantage? If you move out, you get the increase; if you stay, your taxes go up.

9. Who will occupy the new homes?—Upper income, seasonal residents seeking a private community. How does the village feel about these new residents?
10. If you grow the "tails" of the community, the center never gets developed.
11. Based on current demographic projections, with the new development, you would not have enough water for fire protection.
12. During the summer, are you prepared to handle two hundred to nine hundred additional cars per day?

I thought Jack's presentation was a compelling indictment of unplanned growth and a warning to think about these decisions carefully. Amazingly, some village officials left that meeting believing he had endorsed the annexation! Those must have been officials who'd already made up their minds. Luckily, we did not need to convince a majority of the board, or I would have been totally discouraged. We needed three "no" votes, and, for those board members with open minds, Jack's presentation was compelling evidence against rushing to annexation.

The second time we used an expert for Fischer Creek was when we brought in Jeff Pagels, the community liaison from the Wisconsin Department of Natural Resources, to speak at a plan commission meeting. The chairman of the plan commission was furious that we had made the request—he called me and said, "Why don't you go back where you came from?!"—but he did put Jeff on the agenda.

At that time, the Friends had begun to discuss the possibility of making the land a park, but village officials had serious doubts that this was a credible option. Jeff spoke about the State of Wisconsin's Knowles-Newlson Stewardship Program, which granted funds for the purchase of land for conservation purposes. Jeff described the DNR's long-standing interest in the Fischer Creek parcel and the history of negotiations with the landowner. Jeff explained that the DNR could potentially provide 100 percent of the appraised value of Fischer Creek. He left everyone with the impression that we could make this happen.

Jeff's presentation was critical in helping create a viable, alternate scenario—that of Fischer Creek in conservation and open to the public. Rolf Johnson had espoused this vision for the land, but Jeff made it a realistic possibility. This proved to be critical in our defeating the annexation. Several board members were willing to give us some time to see if we could pull off the purchase.

Find the sensitivities.

The reality is that some people in local government are convinced by factors other than pure reason, such as:

1. They do not want to look stupid.
2. They do not want to spend money or be responsible for liabilities.
3. They do not want to be sued.
4. They do not want bad publicity.
5. They *do* want to be reelected.

Your tactics can address some or all of these vulnerabilities.

Looking stupid

For Fischer Creek, we brought in reams of material, cited outside experts, and raised numerous questions about the costs and effects of the proposal. Politicians were looking more and more like they did not know the consequences of the proposal. We set up a situation in which the cautious, reasonable approach was *not* to annex the land. Government would look stupid—or a least ignorant—if it proceeded in the face of all the material we brought to light.

Spending money

Money became an issue in several respects. The village was concerned about out-of-pocket expenditures, as well as about liabilities for future contingencies. In my experience, local government hates spending money on legal fees. This is often an expenditure that is far more politically sensitive than expenditures on public works projects. Local officials (at least in jurisdictions smaller than the county that do not have their own counsel on staff) resent spending money on legal advice and are even more fearful of a prolonged legal battle or litigation. This concern contributed to our success with Fischer Creek and Hika Conservancy. It can also work to your advantage in that local government may not use its own counsel as much as it should, giving your counsel considerable authority.

We raised the specter of future expenditures in Fischer Creek. Whereas the developer claimed he would pay for everything and there would be no costs to the village, we countered that statement in several ways. First, we brought in extensive evidence from the Urban Land Institute, Dr. Huddleston, and elsewhere as to the long-term costs of development. We also pointed to several failed subdivisions in Cleveland and the mess left for the village in terms of unfinished roads and other liabilities.

Fear of lawsuits

Local officials fear being sued. In a large government, litigation may be viewed as a "cost of doing business," but in smaller communities, the cost in terms of finances and reputation are perceived as great. By bringing in a lawyer who quietly but firmly asserted our legal rights, the proper procedures, and other legal matters, the board may have perceived an implicit threat, which was exactly our intention. For Fischer Creek, the Town of Centerville did threaten, in writing, to sue the village in the event of annexation.

Another benefit of the perceived threat of litigation is that if developers perceive that they may be held up or involved in protracted litigation, the economics of their plans change dramatically. Caution: Do not threaten litigation unless you mean it. I am not advocating litigation as a tactic unless it is undertaken with careful thought of the costs—financial, social, and otherwise. Litigation is serious, expensive, and unpredictable. You give up considerable control over the outcome once you start down this road. Sometimes, litigation may be appropriate or unavoidable. Use it only as a tactic of last resort.

Bad publicity

The fear of bad publicity can also be a powerful deterrent, especially in smaller communities. During the Fischer Creek controversy, local newspapers covered the meetings extensively. Rolf also videotaped the proceedings for use in a future documentary. I believe behavior of public officials at these meetings was tempered because of the presence of reporters and videotapes.

On the other hand, we deliberately avoided the press during our campaign for the Hika Conservancy. In that situation, we believed media coverage would unnecessarily polarize the debate and create less room to maneuver and to effect change. For both Hika and Fischer Creek, however, we encouraged many citizens to attend the meetings and witness the discussions. That most basic form of grassroots activity is indeed effective. Honorable local officials will consider strong feelings from their constituents. The outpouring of concern from residents of the Hika neighborhood was certainly a factor in turning the board toward consideration of conservation. This was not the only factor, of course. For some months, the board pursued development plans in the face of community opposition. However, when the legalities and economics of the project began to change, it was critical that the community expressed itself against condominiums and in favor of preserving the Hika Conservancy land.

Reelection

For Fischer Creek, the old guard wanted to stay in power. That did not cause them to modify their position; rather, it polarized the community on the issue. Village officials chose to rally support for their position, rather than compromise. On the local level, it is not uncommon for people to run for office unopposed, because government service is perceived to be a miserable and thankless job. Land controversies can lead to competition for public office in situations in which local government cannot be changed and must be replaced.

Scenario Three: Vote them out of office.

There comes a time in land battles when you realize that you cannot change the hearts and minds of the people in office. Or you realize that you will need a swing vote. Or you are so frustrated at listening to all these meetings that it becomes less painful to serve than to observe. Or your elected officials are complete idiots. For both Fischer Creek and Hika Conservancy, our tactics included changing the makeup of the board.

For Fischer Creek, we waged a major election campaign. In addition to the referendum on the issue of annexation, we ran a write-in candidate for village president and supported a full slate of candidates for open board seats. The presidential candidate and one trustee were write-in candidates because we had missed the filing deadline for getting on the ballot. Undeterred by the serious impediment of promoting write-in candidates, we campaigned furiously. Our presidential candidate beat the incumbent, and two of our three trustee candidates won.

The candidate for president, Kurt Kaiser, campaigned on his experience as a village trustee (Kurt was one of our three "no" votes on annexation, although he had not been identified with the Friends before the annexation vote) and a platform of common sense, welcoming public input, respecting all points of view, and being a consensus builder. All of the Friends' candidates for village trustee promoted a planning process, called "growth within the balance," and citizen involvement through open meetings. The Friends canvassed every household in the village and distributed its own campaign literature in addition to the literature distributed by individual candidates. This may have been the most heated election Cleveland had ever seen.

By election day, things were starting to get ugly in Cleveland. The village was extremely polarized, and I felt bad for long-time residents like my friends across the street, John and Idell Kirsch. People they had known for years were refusing to speak to them at church and at the local restaurant. The Kirschs' property was vandalized. The Friends distributed lawn signs for its candidates, and a few days later the county sheriff removed them, purportedly because they were in the "right of way." A big supporter of the incumbent village president had sons in the sheriff's department and openly boasted of his "connections." The sheriff's actions infuriated people, and some otherwise quiet supporters castigated the sheriff in person. The signs went back up and stayed up. As a newcomer, I was insulated from the worst of the hostilities. I made many friends through my efforts. I also made a lot of enemies, but these were people I did not know and would never know, so it was not as personal as having old friends turn on me. For the long-time residents, their stand on Fischer Creek was a courageous position that risked the disapproval of friends and family, and disturbed the quiet enjoyment of their homes.

Scenario Four: Long-term change— the planning process

Through your work on a land-use issue, you may become motivated to participate in your community's planning process. Planning is a long-term investment. It will not help on a time-sensitive land battle, unless you can convince people to defer a development decision until the planning process is complete. But land-use plans can and do make for better land-use decisions going forward. In the State of Wisconsin, and around the country, "smart growth" plans are becoming requirements. Many communities now have a legally mandated land-use planning process.

After Fischer Creek, Cleveland engaged in a community-visioning process, assisted by the University of Wisconsin Extension. A few years later, through a grant written by John Kirsch and awarded by the Wisconsin Coastal Management Program, Cleveland and Centerville commenced a joint land-use planning process. That process took three years, but resulted in a joint land-use plan adopted by both village and town. At that time, a joint plan between neighboring government entities was almost unprecedented. Subsequent to the joint plan, Cleveland engaged in a neighborhood planning process, which took the land-use designations of the joint plan and fleshed them out into detailed neighborhood plans. Future land-use decisions could be based on a foundation of careful, thoughtful planning. At times, the land-use planning process seemed unbearably tedious, but the dividends were to be long-term.

When the time came to fight development at Hika Conservancy, Cleveland's land-use plans played a major role. The joint land-use plan designated part of the area as conservancy district. For the remainder of the parcel, condominiums were clearly prohibited, and it appeared that townhouses were also prohibited, although that was not as explicit. Under the Cleveland Neighborhood Plan, however, it was clear that only single-family homes were permitted. Certain plan commission members and village trustees said that they would respect the plans in making development decisions. However, once again not even a majority of local officials opted to respect the land-use plans they had taken years of time and expense to create. The temptation for ad hoc decision making must be enormous for local officials.

But the existence of those plans gave us a strong legal basis for challenging decisions inconsistent with the plans. The threat of that challenge, as much as the plans themselves, deterred the development. The payoff for all those planning sessions was huge in terms of our ability to protect a piece of Lake Michigan shoreline from condominium development.

CHAPTER SEVEN

CONDUCT A MEDIA CAMPAIGN

(Opening Pandora's Box)

In many land battles, the media can be decisive in getting your message out and giving yourselves credibility. Once unleashed, however, the media can be called back only with great difficulty. And no matter what you say to the media, you cannot control what they write or display and cannot control their spin on the issues. Therefore, the media can also do your cause great harm. Before unleashing this powerful force, think carefully about the advantages and disadvantages of bringing your conflict to the public arena.

Do you want publicity?

Before embarking on a media campaign, determine whether publicity will help or hurt your cause, based on all the facts and circumstances of your own situation. As a general matter, for big political battles and big fund-raising projects, we used the media to great advantage. For Fischer Creek, we did not have a choice about some of the coverage because the local press began to attend meetings in Cleveland and talked to the developers and Cleveland officials. Therefore, our consideration was how to make the publicity as effective as possible, not whether or not we wanted the publicity. As it turns out, we thought media coverage would benefit us in many ways, so we were not faced with the difficult task of turning off the publicity.

When the other side starts to use the media, you may want to answer in kind. But think about whether this will help or hurt your strategy in the long run. There may be situations in which media attention will not help your cause. Will media attention entrench and polarize the sides? Will it bring out contrary positions in a way that gives them more credibility? For Point Creek, we actively engaged the media as much as possible, with certain exceptions. There were a couple of specific situations during the Point Creek campaign in which we avoided publicity because we thought it could backfire. Later on in this chapter, I discuss several situations in which we tactically decided NOT to seek publicity for just these reasons. The point is: Think about what you are doing and how it will affect your strategy before calling in the media.

The benefits of media coverage

In the right circumstances, media coverage can provide help and opportunity. In smaller communities, local papers love these stories, which provide interest and controversy in often-dull times. A sympathetic reporter can do more to get your story out than weeks of phone calls, leaflets, and meetings.

Press coverage can also give you and your group credibility. In government meetings, local officials and the developer were in the front sharing the floor and the table, while citizens were in the back, relegated to a short public comment period from the back of the room. Rolf understood this dynamic well, and always walked to the front of the room and spoke from there. The media can make you an equal with the developer and government.

At the beginning of the Fischer Creek campaign, we were that "small group of dissident citizens" (as someone was quoted in the newspaper), dismissed to the back of the room. But as the media coverage gained momentum, the story became Developer versus Friends of Fischer Creek. The press gave us equal standing with the developer. We increased our credibility and momentum, and we continually gained more supporters and greater strength throughout the battle. We also wore down the developer and maneuvered him into making mistakes, some of them public and on the record.

As soon as the developer starts talking to the press, he creates opportunity for you. Read and cherish the developer's statements because you will be able to use them to your advantage over time. We accumulated the Fischer Creek developer's statements in the press and in his written submissions to the village. Then we began pointing out his inconsistencies and changes in position. For example, the developer tried to influence the board by stating how much Cleveland would benefit from the new residents' shopping and seeking services in the village. However, when faced with concerns about increased traffic from residents, the developer also said that they would route the traffic to the north around Cleveland. In selling the credibility of his development, the developer had stated that he had an agreement with the Sheboygan Marina and the American Club in Kohler and that residents of the development would probably do their shopping and obtain their services in Sheboygan. Remind me again: How will Cleveland benefit from new customers for shopping and services?

As we emphasized the developer's own inconsistencies, his credibility diminished and his frustration grew. The more frustrated he got, the more he reacted with aggression and desperation, and the more mistakes he made. We treated his every mistake as an opportunity to undermine his statements and credibility further.

Types of media coverage

Think about all kinds of media coverage. Some types are listed below; perhaps you can think of others in your community.

1. *Newspaper articles.* Newspaper coverage, the backbone of a media campaign, can keep your issue alive. Because you are the ones creating and nurturing the issue, news coverage is often beneficial to you. Reporters may cover certain meetings as a matter of course, but call the papers to make sure someone will be there. Don't assume you will have press coverage just because a reporter has attended in the past. Or contact local newspapers and request coverage at certain meetings or events. Nurture a relationship with one or more friendly reporters. Reporters love sources they can rely upon who will review their stories before going to press and who can describe personalities and politics off the record. One reporter routinely called late at night to read

his copy to me before going to press, so that I could review it for accuracy. Those late-night phone calls gave me the opportunity to ensure a balanced and accurate presentation. You are enmeshed in a story—but a reporter will not have the same level of understanding of archaic ordinances and local personalities. If you want coverage, make it easier for newspapers by helping their reporters. Papers typically choose what to cover and what to run. Give them reasons to choose you.

2. *Press releases.* You can issue press releases to the media. Your coverage will usually be in the form of newspaper articles but could be in other media, such as local radio. With press releases, you are controlling the story to a greater degree. Some publications will use all or part of a press release verbatim, so you can also control the tone and spin of the coverage.

3. *Letters to the editor.* This is another good way to get your message out, more or less in your own words. With Fischer Creek, various supporters supplied a constant stream of letters and guest editorials. We countered any pro-development pieces, and continually put forth our own agenda and concerns in addition to the substantial reporting coverage we were receiving.

4. *Editorials.* If you can get supporting editorials, these are a wonderful form of media coverage. The *Sheboygan Press* ran an editorial in November 2000 supporting our efforts to save Point Creek. During our frantic search for donations to meet the West Foundation two-for-one matching challenge grant, the paper endorsed our fund-raising campaign, provided details about where to send money, and further supported our efforts to create a fifteen-hundred-acre "natural zone" midway between the cities of Sheboygan and Manitowoc on the watersheds along Lake Michigan. We couldn't buy that publicity! One can never quantify the effect of such publicity, but the editorial did appear about a month before we received a $200,000 anonymous donation. The editorial helped us as we solicited donations from other public and private sources, and it became a cornerstone of our grant applications and fund-raising materials.

5. *Radio.* In addition to radio news, many local stations have talk

programs on which guests discuss local issues. Rolf and I appeared on Manitowoc radio's "Morning Show" and discussed our efforts to save Point Creek during the hour-long news, talk, and call-in show. One direct benefit of that appearance was that the moderator for the day was the director of the Manitowoc Chamber of Commerce. When she heard about our efforts, she invited us to insert our materials into the regular chamber mailing to members for only the cost of our printing. Information about Point Creek and our fund-raising appeal reached over seven hundred local businesses and individuals for less than $150.

6. *Television.* At the time Fischer Creek became a new state-owned conservation area, Green Bay television filmed a clip on site for their evening news. After the Fischer Creek campaign concluded, a private foundation commissioned a documentary on Great Lakes conservation efforts, and Fischer Creek was one of four featured stories. Wisconsin Public Television broadcast the program. The documentary came after the fact and did not help the Fischer Creek efforts, but it gave us credibility in our future work.

Find a "media personality."

Who in your leadership circle has a good media presence? Has anyone developed a good relationship with the media? If the media finds someone they like to cover, go with it. In our case, it was Rolf Johnson, known as "Wisconsin Johnson" from previous public and radio appearances for the Milwaukee Public Museum. Rolf had significant media experience from his job, had a winning presence, and was enormously articulate. The media darling may not be the person who works the hardest. Put your ego aside in the name of the cause. Yes, sometimes it rankles that people behind the scenes are doing a lot of the work and one person is up there getting the glory. But for the sake of success, try not to let it distract you from getting to your strategic goal. Long after the media attention fades, you will take pride and comfort in your achievement. The people who matter will know your contribution, starting with yourself, your family, and your close friends.

The media likes sizzle.

In terms of working style, I tend to be more steak and less sizzle. The fact is: The media loves sizzle and does not always care about the steak. At the time of Fischer Creek, I was too lawyerly and too literal to make good headlines. I was awash in facts, strategy, and the law, but it was Rolf who articulated a vision and made headlines. Rolf was front-page news, with full color pictures to boot. In January of 1995, Rolf called a press conference to announce that his family was putting their 155-acre farm into a conservation easement. He made headlines. Eight years later, the easement still wasn't done, but Fischer Creek did get done, largely through Rolf's efforts.

I learned a lot from Rolf. To mobilize the public and press you have to think BIG. If you have a vision or dream for your community, the press wants to hear it. You have to capture people's hearts and minds before you can convince them on the specifics. Be careful, though. You don't want to create a target for the other side and you don't want to distract from your core issues.

At the meeting of the DNR board to approve funding for Fischer Creek, one board member asked whether we were going to come back and ask for more money to buy other parcels for this fifteen-hundred-acre biological island. Rolf took a breath and I knew that he was about to launch into a speech. I jumped to the microphone and said, "No!" It was obvious to me that the DNR board was concerned about future payments, about what they were getting into. "No" was the only acceptable answer to get our funding approved, and that was the answer they got. There's a place for sizzle and a place for steak. Make sure you know the difference.

Media coverage may hurt your cause.

For Hika Conservancy, we were trying to change the hearts and minds of a few board members concerning the long-term value of keeping a small piece of the lakeshore undeveloped for conservation and public access. We believed that with further education and time, several board members would come round to our position. We did not want to polarize the sides into entrenched "for" and "against" camps, and we wanted to give public officials the opportunity to ponder, ask, and come round to another point of view in private. In our estimation, publicity would have made it more difficult for those officials to change their minds. Media coverage would mean that reporters would ask people to explain their position. As people justified their initial vote, we were afraid that they would become more entrenched, start to "believe their own press releases," and find it harder to change their position down the road.

Also, because Cleveland generated so much publicity with the Fischer Creek controversy, the community was still sensitive about publicity. We did not want to evoke comparisons with Fischer Creek and were afraid that any media publicity would invariably do that. We were lucky in that local papers were not routinely covering Cleveland's meetings at the time of the Hika Conservancy debate. An eager reporter might have heard the citizen input and created a front-page controversy. As to matters within our control, it was purely a judgment call as to whether media coverage would help. In the case of Fischer Creek, certain votes on the board were a given and others were undecided, and we thought we could change some minds with an intense education campaign and public pressure. Media helped us get the word out and keep getting it out. We also concluded that focusing outside attention on the Cleveland board would help our cause, and the media helped bring the matter to the attention of regional and state organizations.

In the Hika Conservancy effort, rather than working for one key vote like we did for Fischer Creek, we prepared for a longer campaign involving a series of votes on related issues. We were trying to make it as easy as possible for board members to change their votes over time without embarrassment or publicity. Also, we had effectively reached the local Hika neighborhood through leaflets and personal contacts. We did not need the press to reach our constituency. Had the village started down a different path, such as by illegally approving a zoning change, we undoubtedly would have used the media as a powerful tool to get the village to reverse itself. Ultimately, whether or not to seek publicity is a subjective determination based on your gut feeling about what will work in your community.

We used as much media coverage as we could get to keep Point Creek alive as an initiative. We issued press releases upon the award of the challenge grant and upon our meeting the challenge grant, and issued another press release when we had put our financing package together. In between these "newsworthy" events, we encouraged feature articles about the scientific and scenic value of the property and invited reporters to scheduled walks of the land with scientists and local university deans. Because of the involvement of three universities, we encouraged coverage for "education" as well as for conservation. The press gave us credibility in our efforts to save the parcel, got the word out to potential donors and partners, and built community support that would have helped us if we ever had to become adversarial and challenge development of the site. We used press clippings prominently in presentations to potential donors, and I had the impression the clippings made our efforts more credible—the message being, "We are real and we are big."

When to avoid publicity

At one stage in the Point Creek process, however, we deliberately avoided the press. Here's the story that gave rise to that decision: Our grant application with the Department of Natural Resources was ranked number one in the state for the Urban Green Space Program, and the DNR provisionally awarded us $600,000. Because of the size of the grant (over $250,000), it had to be approved by the Joint Finance Committee of the Wisconsin state legislature.

The timing could not have been worse. The Joint Finance Committee got the request in the middle of intense, partisan wrangling over the state's huge budget deficit. Our grant request was coming from the prior year's budget and that money was already allocated, but several Republican members of the committee objected to the allocation. We were never sure exactly why—perhaps as a bargaining chip with state Democrats over the size of future stewardship fund allocations, perhaps out of genuine interest in reviewing the request more thoroughly, or perhaps for other political reasons.

We had a difficult seller to manage and a firm closing deadline to meet. The landowner was adamant about not providing an extension and vowed to walk away permanently if we missed the closing date. We were faced with the problem of how to blast our allocation out of Joint Finance when everything else in the entire state budget was also on hold. We distinguished our allocation as being "different" — with $800,000 in federal funds on the line and another $500,000 in private donations, we heralded our effort as a model public/private partnership for stewardship. The state was getting a $1.9 million asset for $600,000. We mounted an intense lobbying effort at all levels. Grassroots supporters wrote, phoned, and e-mailed. Several major donors to the state Republican party were also large donors to our project, and they agreed to speak with important members of the legislature as well. We brought in the governor's office, which took up the cause but had somewhat limited power with a recalcitrant legislature.

We actively debated whether to go to the press with our dilemma. We had received consistent, positive coverage throughout the two-and-a-half-year effort to save Point Creek and considered whether publicity on this eleventh-hour obstacle would help us. On balance, we decided the risks were too great. We thought the money should be released and there was no better project in the state than ours. However, at that time, every major constituency was facing budget cuts—the university, the corrections system, local government, police, fire, parks. Everybody was at risk. Whereas media coverage might have put more pressure on the objecting legislators, we also feared publicity could create a backlash from a lot of people who wanted the money for other programs.

Although we had been keeping local reporters informed of events along the way, we never told them about the holdup in the state capital, and we asked our supporters not to talk to the press. We did manage to dislodge the funding at the last minute, so I guess our assessment was correct. If we had not succeeded, we might have changed our minds and used the media as a last-ditch effort, or maybe not. We will never know, just as you may never know if your strategy was the best one.

The media campaign for Fischer Creek

After the annexation vote, one of the developers congratulated us on our media campaign. He asked who ran it. At the time, being new to grassroots campaigns, I didn't know we had a "media campaign." From my vantage point, we tried to get some good publicity. At the time, I never thought of it in terms of a "media campaign." I am more sophisticated now and can apply the right label to the activity. I doubt that that would have changed the essence of what we did, however.

From September through December of 1994, local newspapers printed more than thirty articles about the fight for Fischer Creek. The Sheboygan and Manitowoc newspapers had reporters at almost every public meeting. The developer talked to the press on several occasions. We always countered immediately. If the developer said he was making concessions and setting aside fifty acres, we pointed out that the fifty acres were all mandatory setback and non-buildable anyway, so the developer was actually giving us nothing. If the developer said that he wanted to create a "beautiful place," we said the place was already beautiful.

Our cause was the subject of five editorials in the *Sheboygan Press,* as well as several editorials in the *Manitowoc Herald.* For several months, the papers simply reported the political controversy. Then, after the developers threatened the Friends with a SLAPP suit, the first editorial appeared. This is a good example of how a developer responded to pressure by lashing out in a way that ultimately hurt him. The developer obviously had no effective strategy for managing the community's objections.

The following are the headlines and a brief summary of the content of each editorial run in the *Sheboygan Press.* I hope that these will give you some ideas to present to your local media for editorials supporting your cause.

Threats won't work in Hika Cove debate. Editorial commending the courage of the Friends and criticizing developers for strong-arm tactics in threatening the Friends with a lawsuit if they continued their public objections to the development.

Hika Cove proposal needs more study. Editorial stating that the decision on a matter this complex should not be rushed and urging village to use outside experts to answer numerous questions. This editorial worked perfectly with our strategy of delay.

Voters should decide the Hika Cove issue. Editorial advocating that village board members vote against annexation and let the citizens vote on the matter in the referendum.

Show your support for new state park. Editorial asking people to contact the Manitowoc County Board, the state DNR, and the governor to support the purchase of Fischer Creek as a new state park.

Fischer Creek shows what citizens can do. Editorial summarizing the history of the Fischer Creek controversy and lauding citizen involvement.

The final words of the last editorial are just as relevant today: "May it serve as an inspiration to every citizen who thinks his or her views can't be made to count."

CHAPTER EIGHT

FUND-RAISING

(Money Makes the World Go 'Round)

Involved citizenship is expensive.

Standing up for what you believe can be expensive. As you engage in the process of fighting development, you are going to need money and resources. Apart from the opportunity costs of spending time on a land battle instead of on other things, you will also incur out-of-pocket expenses when investigating and organizing a land-use battle.

From the very start, you will be paying for such things as phone calls, photocopying, printing, and faxes. You may need to hire a lawyer, either to protect your rights, delay action on the land, litigate, or negotiate purchase terms. You may decide immediately or down the road that purchasing the property is your best strategy, in which case you will need to raise the purchase price. Whether it is relatively small expenses or enormous sums, you should decide how much of your own money you want to contribute, how you will raise money, and how you are going to process donations. My experience is that for smaller expenses, the leadership circle paid up.

Helping keep costs down is the fact that computer literacy has come a long way since the early 1990s, and now a lot more of your work can be done via e-mail and the Internet. However, although some expenses may be lower than they were a decade ago, the expenses are still there.

As you begin to develop a strategy and promote your cause, you may see additional expenses. For example, Friends of Fischer Creek faced the cost of getting aerial photos taken. Aerial pictures are a wonderful way to see the land configuration, development patterns, and open space. One picture may be worth a thousand words in making your case for conservation. For Fischer Creek, we raised money from supporters for flight time in order to take our own aerial photographs. I was skeptical at first, as it seemed like a big expense of questionable value, but Rolf insisted we do it and he was right. We benefited greatly from taking those pictures. In an aerial view, we could see finger dunes running east and west perpendicular to the Lake Michigan shoreline in a highly unusual formation. We could also see the urban sprawl heading up the lakeshore like a wayward tentacle, with huge open spaces in central Cleveland. Mostly, we could see the majesty of the site, with Fischer Creek winding toward magnificent Lake Michigan. The pictures moved the debate from the realm of partisan local politics and onto a regional level.

Today, the Manitowoc County Planning Department has aerial photos of the entire county on computer, and we might get what we need from them or from another regional planning group. You can also download aerial photos from the Internet, although the scope and quality may not be adequate to meet your needs. Whether for aerial photographs or something else, try to weigh the costs and benefits as best you can but factor into the decision the knowledge that there is probably some financial help out there if you need it.

Paying for a lawyer

You may not need counsel. Or you may need a lawyer and be lucky to have your lawyer donate her time. However, many people find that they need and will have to pay for a lawyer. As soon as you are responsible for legal bills, expenses have moved out of the range of "incidental."

Your first issue in retaining a lawyer is deciding who the client is. Is it you, individually? A group comprising you and several others? A more formal group? I've seen it done all ways. For Fischer Creek, the client was the Friends of Fischer Creek. Although John Kirsch signed the engagement agreement with counsel, we decided that I would be counsel's sole contact. I served as the one control point in the group.

For Hika Conservancy, Otto and Laurel Wimpffen personally retained a lawyer and were solely responsible for legal bills. For Point Creek, Sheboygan Area Land Conservancy was the client and I was once again the contact. But whether you are personally liable for legal fees or a group is liable, you face similar issues in raising the money to pay the bills.

How to raise money for legal fees and other expenses

The easiest way to raise money is to ask for it. Especially for incidental expenses, people may not be aware of the costs involved. It has been my experience that supporters are often willing to cover incidental expenses if they are told what is needed. A supporter may make a general offer of money and support. Take that person up on it! It is a way for people to feel they are helping and involved, especially if they are not permanent residents or do not have the time or energy to attend meetings or otherwise participate. Personally, I hate asking people for money. But by the time I'm writing my fourth personal check for expenses, it gets easier to ask.

You can also ask people to make "in kind" contributions. Over the years, for example, we received sign space on a marquee, free mailing from the chamber of commerce, banking services, printing, office help, artwork, and food. Once again, it never hurts to ask.

As for other fund-raising methods to cover incidental expenses, I have no magic solution. The familiar fund-raising techniques used for PTA, church, and service organizations work here as well. In addition to raising cash, the right fund-raising event can also be an opportunity for coalition building. A barbecue can get people together, raise money, and build spirit. I'm a firm believer in the principle that people are much more likely to participate if they are having fun. At one potluck party for Fischer Creek, we had a silent auction and sold hats and T-shirts with our logo. One of our supporters wrote an original song and played it. We had an impromptu sing-along. One of the local radio stations even played the song, so we got some great media coverage too. We did not raise enough money to buy the land that way, but it certainly helped with legal bills and other expenses. We left a bit richer, financially, as well as more energized to continue the fight.

Getting organized for fund-raising

If you are starting to raise money for incidental expenses and counsel, you must address some threshold organizational issues. To whom do donors write checks? Where should checks be sent? Who will handle the money? Will acknowledgments be sent? How formally this is done will depend in part on how much money you are raising as well as how wide you cast your net. The simplest fund-raising scenario is casual, with a few people chipping in to defray expenses. In that case, people can write a check or give some money to an individual and be done with it.

For Fischer Creek, we were looking at expenses and legal bills in the $10,000–$12,000 range. One of our supporters worked at the local bank, and she facilitated our opening a free checking account in the name of Friends of Fischer Creek. People deposited donations directly to our account or wrote a check to Friends of Fischer Creek for one of our leadership circle to take to the bank. (If you do plan on acknowledging donations, make sure you have a system in place to avoid embarrassing slips. I say this from painful experience.) John Kirsch and I were joint signatories on the checking account, which was used mainly for payment of legal fees. Even after we had an account and were raising money, I covered most of my expenses during the battle, and the Kirschs covered most of theirs. As signers for the checking account, we both bent over backward to avoid even the appearance of impropriety in our handling of the money.

Understanding the issues that accompany fund-raising

Back in 1994 and 1995, when we were fighting for Fischer Creek, we were probably naive about raising money. We had an urgent need and did what we had to do to save the land. We never took the time to research the law or our own potential liability concerning our raising and handling the funds used to pay our lawyer and other expenses. I do not advocate this approach and probably would never repeat it.

You would be well advised to find out if laws regulate your fund-raising activity. There may be restrictions on soliciting funds and on lobbying, and perhaps regulations on how you handle donated funds. There are election laws concerning making donations to and campaigning for a candidate or slate of candidates. Federal tax laws and regulations determine whether a donation is tax-deductible. As a general matter, for a donation to be deductible, it has to be to a "qualified" organization, sometimes known as a "501(c)(3) organization," so named for the section of the federal tax code under which not-for-profit organizations qualify. These organizations have strict restrictions on lobbying activity. If lobbying is one of the significant activities of the organization, it will not qualify for 501(c)(3) status. (The above statements are gross generalizations about a highly complex subject, so please consult your accountant or tax adviser to learn how these rules apply to your specific situation, and for guidance on your own state's laws.)

If you are raising money for a land purchase, fund-raising issues will have to be addressed precisely and correctly. For purposes of raising enough money for incidental expenses and legal fees from friends and neighbors, some informality may be appropriate. A certified public accountant who is treasurer of a community group may have a different comfort level (and very different risk profile) than you or me. Consult your own advisers and conscience and devise a solution that works for you. However, as soon as you contemplate fund-raising from foundations, the government, or wealthy individuals, you must be organized and meet strict legal criteria.

"Let's buy the property": Embarking on a major fund-raising campaign

All three of my land battles started with a few citizens challenging a local development decision. With Fischer Creek, we challenged village annexation of the land; with Point Creek, we challenged the county's granting a variance for a long cul-de-sac; with Hika Conservancy, we challenged a proposed zoning change for condominiums, then one for townhouses. Although these three land battles started at different places, they all converged on the same conclusion: Purchase of the land is the only way to protect it permanently. Purchase prices for the three parcels ranged from $530,000 to $1.9 million.

As soon as you find yourself looking at raising funds of that size, you know you are not going to succeed with bake sales and barbecues. For these princely sums, you will need some combination of public money, private foundation grants, and significant donations from individuals. In order to raise money successfully from these sources, you have to be organized and aggressive and distinguish yourselves from other projects competing for the same dollars.

You may be able to raise public money by convincing the local unit of government to purchase the property, either out of its ordinary revenues or through a bond offering. Even if the spirit is willing, the budget usually won't permit a big expenditure at the local level. It is not unheard of, however, and is certainly worth investigating.

You may also be able to obtain a line enumeration in the state or federal budget for allocation of money toward purchase of that particular parcel. This is accomplished by lobbying. For example, the Trust for Public Lands has had some success in raising money for land acquisition through lobbying for line-item additions in the National Oceanic and Atmospheric Administration (NOAA) budget. In order to obtain purchase money through lobbying, you need to get help from conservationists who are knowledgeable about all the potential sources of money, and you need to work any political connections in the state and federal legislatures as well.

Funding through budget enumeration is an uphill battle, however. An organization like Trust for Public Lands has as its mission helping grassroots conservation efforts, but the number of groups it can help is small compared to the number seeking its help. Apart from facing the general problem of tight budgets at all levels of government, you must compete with those conservationists who are in the best position to help you. In other words, any conservation organization with the contacts and ability to help you would likely want to use those contacts and ability to raise money for its own projects. The big conservation organizations, like the Nature Conservancy, have sophisticated systems in place for getting as much of the available public monies as possible. When "Big Conservation" is allied with "Big Government," you may find neither of them about to help you. This is an example of how difficult it is at the grassroots level.

My experience is that, for the most part, politicians stay away from local land-use disputes unless they are jumping on the bandwagon moments before success. (State Senator Jim Baumgart, in Wisconsin, was a notable exception. He interceded several times during the

Point Creek process and was also known as one of the most environmentally responsible members of the state senate. There are politicians like Jim around, but they are the exception rather than the rule. In the election following our acquisition of Point Creek, Jim lost by approximately twenty votes to a Republican challenger.) If you have good contacts, that's great—use them. But most of us will not succeed through lobbying and the legislative budget process. Absent some fortuitous connections with powerful politicians, and the right timing and political climate, this is not a likely source of funding. I personally never had any success financing a project through state or federal enumeration in the budget. Also, this usually takes a long time and is highly uncertain. Most land battles cannot survive an extended timeline. For all these reasons, this chapter will focus on raising money through public and private grants.

Put a structure in place.

Foundations and sophisticated individuals will only make tax-deductible donations. Therefore, you either need to form a 501(c)(3) entity, which is possible but may not be practical within your time frame, or, more likely, find a 501(c)(3) entity that will accept donations on behalf of your land acquisition.

One place to start your search is with a land conservancy (also known as a land trust) serving your region. If you do not know of one, find your statewide umbrella organization for land trusts; it can direct you to the land trust serving your region. If you do not know the statewide umbrella organization, ask persons working for other statewide environmental organizations for the name and contact information for your land trust alliance. A land trust may or may not step in to help you. Some land trusts do not want to purchase property, have specific strategic plans in which they focus on certain activities, or have threshold requirements as to size or dollar value. Others, like the Sheboygan Area Land Conservancy, were flexible in enacting their commitment to conserving land and worked with us to make Point Creek happen.

Absent an available land trust, try another local not-for-profit conservation organization in your region. What you are looking for is pretty basic. You need an organization to set up a program or an account for your land acquisition, process the receipt of donations through their tax-exempt organization, send acknowledgments to donors, and keep records. Essentially, that organization will be putting its name behind you and your activities and adopting you as a program within their activities. Once a relationship is formed, you may be able to help with some of these activities, such as sending acknowledgments under the organization's name. The organization's own advisers will tell them how to structure the relationship within the proper boundaries of its 501(c)(3) status. The work involved is not complicated, if you can sell the organization on helping you.

There are lots of reasons that a land trust or conservation organization might want to help you, in addition to their basic desire to save land. An organization, especially a smaller one, might appreciate the widespread exposure and publicity it derives from your efforts and might find it a fair trade to help process your donations for a publicized land purchase. Many organizations are hungry for new board and committee members. Your group is a new source of people who could fill such positions in the long term. Also, your land acquisition could help implement part of that organization's strategic plan. You could structure the alliance as either a short-term relationship, or anticipate a continuing relationship. See which approach is most appealing.

The other alternative is to use a LUG (local unit of government) to process donations. Some government grants require that a LUG make the application and hold title to the land. If this is the case, that same LUG may also agree to process donations for you. Typically, that task involves the LUG's maintaining a separate account for the land purchase, and receiving donations and crediting them to the separate account. For Hika Conservancy, the Village of Cleveland agreed to perform this role and further agreed that if the land purchase did not occur, the village would return the money to the donors. The village concluded that only basic record keeping and account management were required to manage the job.

How does this work in practice?

For Point Creek, our fund-raising began in the name of the Sheboygan Area Land Conservancy, and SALC received and deposited foundation and individual donations in a separate account. However, as we applied for bigger grants, we learned that the Wisconsin DNR was not comfortable with SALC as the owner of the land; they requested that the deed be held either by an organization that had been around longer or by a LUG. Initially, the SALC board had a strong preference for keeping the land out of the hands of government and hoped that one of the state universities would own the land and meet the DNR's criteria.

Then we learned of one-time federal grants made available by the NOAA being administered by the Wisconsin Coastal Management Program ("Coastal"). Because of a budget compromise in Washington, D.C., that year (during the 2001–2002 grant cycle), almost $6 million was available to the State of Wisconsin for land acquisition and other projects for counties bordering the Great Lakes. The grants were for up to 75 percent of the total project cost. The amount and timing of the grant package were uncanny, given our desperate search for funds. Once again, Point Creek was in the running!

To qualify for the biggest pool of Coastal money, the applicant had to be a LUG. Conserving the land was our foremost mission, so we quickly concluded that partnership with the County of Manitowoc was in fact a splendid idea. We worked through County Planning and Parks Director Mike Demske and the county planning and parks commission. The county was willing to be the applicant (SALC did all the work of completing the application) for the Coastal grant and hold the land, but it did not want the expense or burden of managing the land. We then organized a consortium of three universities that agreed to manage the land. Like the county, the universities were also on tight budgets, and they agreed partly because we anticipated that it would not cost them anything. Much of the land was to be left in its natural state, and we hoped that thinning the dense pinewoods to permit hardwoods' secession would be profitable. The county would oversee the construction of a small parking lot and the demarcation of unpaved foot trails. Ultimately, management of the land fell to a five-party management committee consisting of the three universities, Manitowoc County, and SALC.

He who writes the check controls the project.

Herein lies another important lesson: When you take large sums of money, you must share control of the project. That's a fact of life, and a painful one at times. (Actually, you only lose control of certain aspects of the project, but it *feels* like you've lost control of the whole project.) As it turned out, our fears about working with the county on Point Creek were unfounded. The county was a reasonable and cooperative partner; we all wanted the same ends; and we truly could not have done it without them. The DNR Stewardship Fund and the Coastal grants each had rules and regulations governing the acquisition process and the use of the land acquired through it. That certainly makes sense, because each program was responsible for administering millions of dollars of public funds. But it also means that applicants must comply with two sets of complex, sometimes conflicting, requirements.

Although we had good working relationships with the county during the acquisition process, we were all anxious that the land remain in conservation forever. We wanted to prevent future government from selling or developing the land. For Point Creek, we met this concern by putting a conservation easement on the land. Despite some bureaucratic roadblocks, SALC insisted upon retaining control of this aspect of the acquisition.

SALC adamantly required a conservation easement as a condition to relinquishing the private funds we had raised. The conservation easement runs from the county (the legal owner of the land) to SALC and prohibits development and other various stated activities on the land. The easement gives SALC legal enforcement rights should the terms ever be violated. The fact that SALC had raised the funds and was making a significant contribution to the purchase gave it the leverage to make that demand and see that it stuck.

Relationships matter.

In fund-raising, whether public or private, relationships matter. This is as true for government grants as it is for foundation grants. The government, as an entity, may not be your friend, but you should cultivate friends who work for the government. The Fischer Creek and Point Creek acquisitions were both possible only through government grants. Our success in winning those government grants largely resulted from the help we received from select government servants who believed in the projects and became our internal advocates during the long grant process.

At the DNR, Jeff Pagels nurtured both the Fischer Creek and Point Creek applications for the DNR Stewardship Fund. Jeff helped us consider whether to apply for a grant, and he assisted in every step until we received the check. He advocated for the projects at various levels within the DNR and was instrumental in the high rankings and ultimate awards for both projects. He helped us with technical problems, such as choosing appraisers, timing appraisals and updates, and meeting the requirements for a purchase agreement with the landowner. There are many technical requirements that can disqualify an application if someone is not actively working for the project. Unless one or more employees is vested in your project, it is easier for government to find a reason to deny an application than to put in the work to approve it.

Jeff Pagels even kept us informed of other grant opportunities. He knew, before we did, that the DNR Stewardship Fund would not cover the purchase price and that we needed to show overall financial wherewithal to be seen as competitive by the DNR. For Point Creek, he encouraged us to apply for the Coastal grant and helped us put together the financing package of public and private monies that ultimately enabled the purchase. When applying for a grant, don't just fill out paperwork, then send it in and forget about it. Your chances of success are much higher if you cultivate relationships with people on the inside who can work the application for you.

We had a similar experience with the Wisconsin Coastal Management Program, when we prepared our grant application for Point Creek. We worked closely with the staff in completing the application, and both Jim Langdon and Mike Friis helped immensely as we navigated a bureaucracy subject to both state and federal rules. But we had not cultivated any other relationships at Coastal. We were incredibly lucky that a senior person on the decision-making council, Bill Wiesmueller, believed in the project and kept it alive throughout the application process. In the final round of consideration for the grants, we spent a lot of time with Mike, Jim, and Bill—walking the land; elaborating on the research and educational potential for the site, its value to the public, and the credentials of the management committee; providing background information about Fischer Creek and the history of conservation activism in the community; discussing my credentials and those of our leadership circle; and otherwise building our credibility.

We asked for—and ultimately received—the second highest grant in the Coastal program, $800,000. The only higher award went to the City of Milwaukee. Coastal took a big risk by supporting our acquisition. Remember, we were competing against large cities, the DNR (which itself applied for numerous Coastal grants), and established conservation organizations and regional planning groups. A grant of that size, made to a group as small and unknown as SALC, could only be secured through our convincing the people at Coastal of our seriousness, commitment, and credibility. These are traits that cannot be measured in a formal application but have to be imparted through relationship building. The people at Coastal bent over backward to be fair and to give the smaller, unsophisticated applicant an equal chance against the larger municipalities and the DNR. We were incredibly lucky that the Coastal agency had its employees and its council willing to work harder to find a way to approve a difficult application.

When you apply for grants, it is important to understand these dynamics. You are competing with many other worthy projects. You need to give staff reasons to support your project over others and you need to nurture advocates on the inside.

Applying for public grants to purchase land

Each public-grant program will have its own detailed requirements. Review those requirements carefully, especially as to eligibility, valuation, and supporting documentation. The grant may state which factors earn points and how bonus points are earned. Study this carefully and write your grant with a focus on the point criteria. See if you can get a copy of a grant application for that program and review the substance and format of a "successful" grant. Sometimes granting agencies will give seminars on how to apply for the grant. Find out if one is offered and attend. These seminars are informative and give you a chance to meet some of the people processing the grants.

It is possible to succeed as a novice. The first grant I wrote was the Coastal application for Point Creek. I worked hard and carefully on the application; I had the benefit of reviewing the application to the DNR Stewardship Fund for the same project, prepared by Rolf Johnson, an experienced grant writer; and I did my homework by carefully researching existing studies to accumulate scientific and public-sector support for the acquisition.

All grants have different requirements and priorities, but as a general rule we assumed that "more is better." Mike Demske put it well when he advised me, "Usually we just assume that the heaviest application wins." Accordingly, we included many attachments and citations, making for a heavy (and, we hoped, substantively impressive) submission. A summary of the types of issues we addressed on the Coastal grant follows; it may demystify the process and give you a practical example of how these grants work. The Coastal grant involved federal money administered by the State of Wisconsin. Accordingly, the Coastal program had two sets of procedural requirements to rationalize and administer.

Scoring of the Coastal grant application gave greatest weight to a project's effect on coastal resources. Throughout the application we emphasized the threat of immediate development of this coastal area. The landowner said he was on the verge of developing, and we could show that this was no empty threat, given the sprawl working its way up the Lake Michigan shoreline from Chicago to Green Bay. We had particular development pressures in the region because of the addition of several championship golf courses a few miles down the road. After making our case that the threat of development was immediate, we discussed the negative effects of development. We used examples such as the effect on the groundwater of putting septic systems on the tall coastal bluffs. We cited a scientific study, funded by Coastal, describing the danger that private septic systems posed to groundwater quality and bluff stability.

We emphasized other topics that the grant application listed as earning points: "Whether the project addressed high-priority needs as identified in state-recognized plans," and the extent to which the project "leverages technical or financial resources." I was not sure exactly what qualified as a "state-recognized plan" so I found support for the Point Creek Watershed Initiative in as many state and local plans and studies as I could and cited them all in the application.

As to the "leverage" issue, we focused on two points. First, we discussed how the acquisition was part of the same overall vision as the acquisition of Fischer Creek (a $1.3 million investment in coastal conservation), as well as several adjoining pieces of land in conservation. Including the thirty-nine-acre Point Creek parcel, the contiguous land in conservation would be about 140 acres. Including the Fischer Creek parcel, one mile south and not contiguous, there were about three hundred acres in conservation. We argued that the whole was indeed greater than the sum of the parts, and that this qualified as "leverage" for points in the application. Second, we emphasized how this acquisition would implement recommendations made in other plans and studies funded by Coastal. In that way, we saw this as leverage of Coastal's own past investments. We learned that Coastal liked to authorize projects that had been recommended by previous studies funded by them, so we emphasized every possible link between the Point Creek acquisition and previous work funded by Coastal.

With some digging, I found a number of authorities that supported the Point Creek acquisition. I knew of few of these resources when I started the application, but through talking to people and doing Internet research, I uncovered the following:

1. The Wisconsin DNR had issued a Land Legacy Study, which identified Point Creek as a priority site.
2. Manitowoc County, with a grant funded by Coastal, had commissioned a study of coastal wetlands of Manitowoc County, conducted by scientists at the University of Wisconsin in Madison. The Coastal Wetlands Study had useful information about the importance of the Point Creek site and the dangers of developing it.
3. The Village of Cleveland and Town of Centerville had prepared a joint land-use plan, also funded with a Coastal grant, that designated part of the tract as an environmental preserve.
4. The DNR had issued the Data Compilation and Assessment of

Coastal Wetlands of Wisconsin's Great Lakes, which listed Point Creek as an "ecologically significant site" and as a "primary site" for Lake Michigan wetlands.

5. The DNR had awarded a River Protection Grant to the Fischer Creek Alliance (a program of SALC) for producing a strategic plan identifying priority ecosystems in the Point Creek and Fischer Creek watersheds.

6. The Manitowoc County Defined Environmental Corridors Map showed the entire Point Creek property as an environmental corridor.

7. The Biological Inventory of Kingfisher Farm, a study performed by scientists at the University of Wisconsin in Green Bay, identified a multitude of plant and animal species at the Kingfisher Farm site, which is directly adjacent to the Point Creek site.

8. The DNR State of the Lakeshore Basin Report discussed priorities for management and protection of natural resources in the basin, which includes all of Manitowoc County. We were able to show that acquisition of the Point Creek site addresses six out of eight of the highest priority concerns identified in the report.

9. The Manitowoc County Park and Open Space Plan recommended purchase of a county Park site adjacent to Lake Michigan between the Village of Cleveland and the City of Manitowoc.

Citing so much source material removed the application from the realm of a subjective recommendation to that of a decision backed by objective scientific fact and supported by government. I amassed most of this information through my own digging. I called people at County Parks and Planning and went there to look at documents; I got a lot of the Wisconsin DNR information from their Web site. There may be more out there to support your efforts than you realize, if you look and ask.

We enclosed numerous exhibits with the grant application. The grant required several items, such as a certified resolution from the applicant LUG and an appraisal. We also included the marketing material we had prepared for fund-raising; lists of donors; supporting letters from universities, conservation organizations, and government; documentation relating to the landowner's request for variance and grant of the variance; aerial maps and plat maps; color photographs of the property; and press releases and all our press clippings.

That year, Coastal also gave bonus points for building partnership alliances, designing educational strategies, and encouraging coast-wide projects. Here is where a lot of our grassroots efforts paid off. We used our letters of support from organizations and universities to show our partnership alliances. It was easy to make a case for an educational strategy when we had supporting letters from three universities. As well, promoting Rolf's vision for a larger watershed, and identifying those lands in conservation south of Point Creek made a case for a coast-wide strategy. If you are a bit creative, you can marshal a lot of your previous work to justify a grant application.

The life cycle of a grant: Point Creek

Prepare yourself for managing the entire life cycle of your grant. It is not so simple as filling out a form and waiting for Ed McMahon to arrive at your door, check in hand. For Point Creek, we received two publicly funded grants, one from the DNR Stewardship Fund, and one from the Wisconsin Coastal Management Program. Both grants required significant time commitments *after* the application had been submitted.

We filed the application for the stewardship grant on April 28, 2001. After Rolf Johnson prepared the lengthy application, Jeff Pagels, our community liaison at the DNR, informed us of technical problems with the application. We needed to have our appraisal updated. Also, the DNR was concerned that we did not have an option or purchase agreement with the seller of the land. Ultimately, we did not negotiate a land contract until almost a year later, and it was only through Jeff's internal advocacy that we were able to remain competitive. Luckily, Jeff understood that we were working with a difficult and inflexible landowner and had a better chance of arriving at an acceptable price by waiting him out. In terms of valuation, the DNR makes its own independent appraisal of each parcel under consideration. During this process, the DNR land-valuation expert questioned the two appraisals we submitted with the application, which showed a difference in valuation of approximately $300,000.

Months later, we were overjoyed to learn that the DNR ranked our application number one in the state for the Urban Green Space Program of the stewardship fund, with a proposed award of approximately $600,000, which was 50 percent of the DNR's appraised value of approximately $1.2 million. After a well-earned celebration, we learned that our troubles were just beginning. First, the application had to pass through several more internal reviews at the DNR. While that in itself might not be cause for worry, during that time the state budget problems worsened and politics began to interfere with the objective ranking process. It became seriously doubtful that there would be any monies available to fund the award. We sweated that out.

Meanwhile, we reached a purchase price with the landowner of $1.9 million and Coastal awarded us a grant of $800,000. We had raised enough in private donations to make up the $500,000 difference between the two grants and the purchase price. We were jubilant!

Not so fast. We learned that the DNR has a practice of not participating in land acquisitions in excess of the DNR's own appraised value—the rationale being that the DNR is a constant purchaser in the land market, and if they pay inflated land values on one purchase it can affect subsequent purchases. So even though the DNR portion of the acquisition was only $600,000, we were in danger of losing their entire grant. Without the DNR's participation, accumulation of the purchase price would be impossible.

We now had to commence an internal lobbying effort at the DNR to have them waive their practice for the Point Creek acquisition. Assisted by people at the Coastal program and by Jeff, we made our case to the DNR. I felt like we were losing control of the project. We had no particular knowledge or expertise about the DNR bureaucracy, or how to affect it. My guess is that something happened in DNR/Coastal politics, but I truly don't know. At any rate, we got the nod from the DNR and breathed a huge sigh of relief.

The sigh of relief did not last long. The final steps in approving the DNR award involved the DNR secretary's making a recommendation for the acquisition to the Joint Committee on Finance of the Wisconsin state legislature. All DNR awards in excess of $250,000 had to pass the Joint Finance Committee. In the past, projects had made it through Joint Finance in a timely fashion. Because we had a partnership using federal funds and substantial private monies, we assumed this would be a "no-brainer" for the committee. But we made that assumption before the 2002 "budget crisis" hit Madison. As our project sat in the DNR secretary's office awaiting recommendation to the legislature, the news from the legislature got worse and worse every day. Try as we might, we could not blast the paperwork from the secretary's desk out to Joint Finance to get the process under way.

Finally, the application made it to the Joint Finance Committee. There is a passive review period of fourteen days, meaning that if no committee members file an objection, the allocation is deemed approved. If an objection is filed, the committee has to vote on and pass the recommendation. On day thirteen of the passive review period, three Republicans objected to the award, including the cochairman of the committee.

We had a firm date in the purchase contract by which we had to close or the sale was off. We had a difficult seller, who was looking for reasons to break the purchase agreement rather than collect his $1.9 million from us. And we had a state legislature that was gridlocked in partisan budget negotiations. We had only two possibilities: Get the objecting committee members to remove their objections, or get the committee to schedule a vote on the allocation.

I had no experience in legislative maneuvering. I also had no idea what would work, so we worked both strategies. In the event of continued delay, our relations with the landowner would be easier if we had a firm date for a committee vote. Developers hate uncertainty. Even if the committee vote followed our scheduled closing date, we thought we would have a decent shot at getting an extension from the landowner. But open-ended uncertainty was the worst possible situation for us. We could not possibly convince this particular landowner to "trust us" given the negotiating history between us.

We got as many people as we could to write, telephone, and e-mail the members of the Joint Committee, especially the objecting members. We also asked some of the wealthy individual and foundation donors to Point Creek to use their contacts in the Republican party to help us. I called the governor's office and found help there, although, given the peculiar state of Republican politics at that time, it was unclear whether Governor McCallum could help us, or whether these objections were done in part to thwart him. (Two days before the committee members filed their objections to Point Creek, the governor had issued a press release announcing the Coastal grant and stating his support for the acquisition at Point Creek. Governor McCallum would suffer embarrassment if the acquisition failed because of objections from his own party.) The governor thus had his own reasons for getting the funds released. The Coastal program worked intensely, as did the DNR lobbyists. I worked day and night, and when there was nothing left to do, I worried day and night.

Meanwhile, our lawyer was working with the landowner. We tried to keep the delay from him as long as possible, but word got out, and then our problems increased. It had taken an unbelievable amount of time, patience, concession, and hand holding to get the landowner to enter into the contract with us. Months of building our credibility were about to be blown. Peter had his hands full managing the landowner and trying to negotiate an extension. I know it doesn't seem rational—why wouldn't the guy give us a little more time with $1.3 million already in escrow and the rest coming sooner or later? It's not rational, but that's what made the landowner so difficult. Finally, the landowner offered us a deal under which he extend our closing date: He wanted a personal meeting with the governor's top aide for the environment, so that he could lobby his own special interests. If we arranged that, he would give us a limited extension on our closing date. My stomach turned at the terms. If we agreed, in my mind we would be "selling" access to the governor in exchange for saving our own project.

The day before our closing deadline, the Joint Finance Committee withdrew its objections. We never had to broker access to the governor—which was a relief—although we were prepared to do it, so I wasn't any happier with myself. We still do not know how or why we succeeded. Certainly, we had strong arguments given that the project was bringing in $800,000 in federal money and $500,000 in private money. The state would be buying a $1.9 million piece of land for $600,000. However, it is my guess that it was influence, not equity, that won the day. Several influential members of the state Republican party were donors, and I believe they spoke to the "right people" on our behalf. But perhaps I am too cynical. By all accounts, our lobbying effort got high marks in Madison for effectiveness and visibility. The Joint Finance Committee released the funds. We were home free!

Or so we thought. As the DNR prepared the final paperwork to release its check, the acquisition had to undergo one more review—this time with the DNR's internal auditors. Even as the check was being cut, the DNR internal auditing department raised questions about whether the site was contaminated, based on several brief comments made in one of the appraisals we had submitted with the application, in which the appraiser noted that several barrels and other items had been dumped on the land. We had a matter of hours to convince DNR internal audit that the site was clean so that our check would be released.

We had never addressed this issue before. Luckily, one person in our small leadership circle, Ron Schaper, was intimately familiar with the site, happened to be available at that moment by e-mail, and could discuss in detail every empty barrel and other object cited. Ron knew that one empty barrel was labeled "tomato paste" (not toxic chemicals) and used as a trash barrel. Ron listed every item that he could remember and explained it to the satisfaction of the auditors. The DNR talked about the possibility of a site inspection. With one call to Mike Demske, we arranged for the county to send a crew the next day to haul away the offending items. I learned later that the DNR auditors tried to have the check recalled, but they were too late. The check made it to escrow and cleared. We later learned that there may have been some internal DNR politics at play in this goal-line stand, and we just happened to be in the way. It was a sobering experience. One or two accountants in the DNR bureaucracy came awfully close to derailing an acquisition that was two and a half years in the making.

We had similar ups and downs with the Coastal grant, although none quite so dramatic. If you decide to apply for public money, understand that it is an active process, right up until the check clears. We probably had a few more bumps in the road than is usual. Like the Boy Scouts, you must be prepared! If you understand the process and are not taken by surprise you will overcome the obstacles and succeed.

Grants from private foundations

For Point Creek, we received $750,000 in donations and pledges, including significant donations from several local charitable foundations. Some of this money was directly linked to Rolf Johnson's credibility and past work with people. This is a prime example of the importance of relationships. In seeking private sponsors, start with local foundations and work from there. You probably have the best chance of success with those foundations that are closest to your community. Foundations that work on the state and even national level offer grants, but it may be hard to acquire them within your time frame, and these funds are even more competitive. "Smaller" and "closer" probably moves faster.

For our largest private donation, the one from the West Foundation, it was our preparation and enthusiasm that convinced the board. Like the Coastal program, the West Foundation decided to take a chance on a project outside its comfort zone. The West Foundation only donates to projects in Manitowoc County, so it was a logical target for Point Creek. However, it had never funded a land acquisition, so Point Creek did not fit its historical profile for grants. Even in Manitowoc County, competition for funds is fierce. The Maritime Museum and the YMCA were both seeking funding, the library had just finished a capital campaign, and many other worthy community organizations needed money.

Nonetheless, we applied. The first thing we did was try, as best as possible, to point out the ways in which the Point Creek acquisition could be seen as consistent with some of the historical priorities of the West Foundation. We emphasized the educational value of the site, especially for children. Next, we insisted on making a presentation to the West Foundation in person, a somewhat unusual request. Because we knew we did not fit the customary profile, we wanted the chance to sell the project and ourselves. We sent a team of three: Rolf, myself, and Mike Sorenson (cochairman of SALC and a certified public accountant). Because the foundation did support museums and educational causes, I made a strong pitch for Point Creek as a living museum. "If we do not save this area now," I argued, "we'll be back in ten years asking for money for a museum describing the habitat we lost along the lakeshore." Rolf's vision, enthusiasm, and experience are unparalleled. He is at his best in this milieu. I was there to give them confidence that the entire acquisition process was tightly controlled and managed. Mike spoke about the history and credibility of SALC and lent assurances that the funds would be handled properly.

A few weeks later we learned the good news and the bad news. The good news was that the West Foundation had awarded us $250,000. The bad news was that the award was a two-for-one matching grant. In other words, if we could raise $500,000 in donations and pledges by the end of the year, West would award us $250,000. True to type, Rolf was elated and I was depressed. He saw the grant and I saw the work. I did not think we had the proverbial "snowball's chance" of meeting the terms of the grant. The strategy of the West Foundation succeeded, however, and we worked tirelessly to bring in the needed match. We got one extension of our deadline from West Foundation but met the challenge a few months later.

I believe that the West Foundation trustees worked with us to find a way to help us succeed because we were local, enthusiastic, and hardworking. As it turned out, our decision to push for a personal presentation worked. Several trustees told us, much later, that they had awarded us the grant largely because they were so impressed with our incredible enthusiasm and commitment. These are factors that will not show in a written application.

Donations from individuals

Fund-raising from individuals can seem like a time-consuming endeavor without much to show for it, but it is important for many reasons. In addition to raising money, it shows both community and individual commitment. There is no better way to prove grassroots support than by pointing to the number of people who send you money.

For Point Creek, the donations from all our local individual donors were not close to totaling one West Foundation grant. However, the broad-based community support added credibility to our cause and depth to our organization. We used this credibility to get larger grants. Also, you never know when you will need grassroots help! When our DNR stewardship grant was held up in committee in Madison, our donor list was the first group we tapped for support. Our donors called, wrote, and e-mailed legislators and helped solicit other individuals to do the same. Ultimately, we were the only stewardship grant in many months to have made it out of committee. No one is quite sure how we did it, but the vocal support of a broad range of donors—from business owners and active Republicans to retired farmers, teachers and active Democrats—did not hurt. We showed bipartisan support and raised the issue from one of playing partisan politics into one of supporting something good for all the people of Wisconsin.

There are no secrets about how to recruit individual donors. We targeted a small number of rich individuals and treated them as "foundations." We sent these individuals the full-color bound brochure that we had prepared for foundations. We gave them a lot more information and personal attention than individuals generally. Our reward was pledges and donations in the $3,000–$50,000 range from about ten wealthy individuals.

For general solicitation of individuals, we sent a one-page information sheet along with a donation form and return envelope. We asked our board members and key supporters each to provide the names of fifteen more people we could solicit. We networked and brainstormed lists of possible donors. We looked at the donor lists at the local art museum and library and got names from there. We inserted information in the chamber of commerce monthly mailing. We encouraged newspaper editorials endorsing the cause and publishing information about how to donate. Seeking individual donations involved a lot of running around and envelope licking. All told, we got more than a hundred individual donors, with donations generally ranging from $25 to $1,000.

Conclusion

If you embark on a major fund-raising campaign, get help from people experienced in fund-raising, from government employees administering grants, and from wealthy and politically connected supporters. Try to get as much time as you can from the landowner for making payments on the land purchase. Major fund-raising is possible, but it takes time to apply for grants and work within the grant cycles of foundations and government. Encourage the landowner and your supporters to be realistic as to how long it takes to raise significant sums of money. Two or more years is a realistic time frame. You will be fighting on two fronts—competing with other worthy projects for limited funds and racing against the clock to raise funds by a certain date. It is more of a marathon than a sprint, so be prepared to go the distance if you want to succeed.

CHAPTER NINE

OPPOSING THE DEVELOPER
(Bluster, Bully, and Bluff)

Dealing with landowner and developer

Friend or foe, the landowner or developer is usually a factor in land battles. In some circumstances, you may be directly battling a developer. This was the case for us with both Fischer Creek and Hika Conservancy. Developers wanted the village to pass annexation or zoning changes to facilitate development, and citizens directly opposed those changes. The battle as to who would prevail with the local government was between the citizens and the developer.

In other circumstances, you may be negotiating with the landowner for purchase of a property. This was the case with Point Creek, where we had protracted negotiations over price and terms, and later with Hika Conservancy, when the developers decided that their best bet was to sell to the village rather than to develop the parcel under the lower-density zoning permitting only single-family homes. You may have a situation in which the landowner is not on the front line. If local government is seeking to make certain annexation or zoning changes, it is likely that a developer or landowner is lurking not far in the background. Look at the economics of the situation—who stands to benefit?—and the hidden interests will be found.

It's about money (not land).

To be successful, you must consider what the landowner or developer wants and how they operate. You won't be far off if you assume that landowners, and especially developers, want as much money as they can get. You may be working with a landowner who has some conservation ethic. In that case, they want fair market value for their land, but may be willing to give you time to raise the purchase price, and might be willing to consider some tax structuring in the transaction. Don't assume they are doing this out of the goodness of their hearts. Sometimes, it is just that from a risk/reward analysis, the conservation purchaser may actually be the better bet for a landowner wanting to cash out. In the case of a non-adversarial landowner, your battle may be more with time and fund-raising than with him.

For the developer, however, it is pretty safe to assume that his sole motivation is money. There are ecologically minded developers. Unfortunately, they are still a small minority and were not involved in Fischer Creek, Point Creek, or Hika Conservancy. If the developer is truly conservation-minded, you probably will not be waging a land battle with him or her. Therefore, the advice in this chapter is geared toward dealing with the typical developer—who wants as much money, in as short a period of time, with as little risk, as possible.

How developers make money

By understanding how developers make money, you can formulate a more effective strategy to defeat development. Identify a developer's weaknesses and use them to your advantage. Key issues to a developer may be timing (such as beginning construction by a certain date), costs, and net revenues. It will help for you to build your own credibility and erode the developer's credibility on a variety of fronts. Obviously, you must assess your own situation, but here are some general points concerning developers:

Developers are highly leveraged. Developers invest as little money as they possibly can. You can use this fact in several ways: (a) Point out how little preparation the developer has done. Is he presenting a generic house design or plat created from a generic computer program? Is he superimposing a suburban plat on a sensitive environmental location? Often, a developer will make a presentation to a local plan commission with as little invested as possible. (b)

Make requests that would cause a developer to spend money. Ask for a preliminary plat, detailed renderings, environmental impact studies, and so on. They hate that. If they balk, you can point to their uncooperativeness as a lack of good faith.

Developers may not own the land. A corollary to the rule that developers do not invest money is that they may not own the land or have an option on the land. If possible, find out their legal relationship, if any, to the parcel. You may be surprised as to who the legal owner is. If you can learn the terms of any option or escrow, you will have a roadmap showing how to defeat the project, because all the important contingencies will be stated. Usually, these terms are confidential, so you may not be able to see them and may have to guess. For Fischer Creek, the purchase money was in escrow, and we surmised that annexation was a condition to release of the escrow. For Hika Conservancy, it appeared that the developers did not have a contingency for needed zoning changes. You may be lucky and learn that developers are speaking for a parcel when they do not have the required ownership interest in the parcel. This may violate local law (which may require that only the landowner can make certain petitions concerning the land). If you discover this, it will make local officials angry and embarrassed, will cast doubt on everything else the developer has said, and will create a rift in the developer/government alliance.

Developers move fast. Developers do not like delay, for a lot of reasons. They do not want to invest money or time in a project that is not offering any return. They do not like uncertainty, because uncertainty equals risk and added costs, and delay adds uncertainty to the outcome. Also, if developers move fast, they are vulnerable to far fewer questions about the project and what is really happening. For all these reasons, delay is often a good tactic for people wanting to stop development. Delay is costly for the developer and gives you time to develop alternate facts, scenarios, and financing.

Developers have no stake in your community. For the most part, developers have no stake in your community. Although this is an obvious point, it is amazing how many people, especially local officials, do not get it. It is especially frustrating to see local officials believe developers and ignore the concerns of taxpaying residents. Sometimes a local farmer or landowner who lives in the community will subdivide a few lots for development but will continue to live in the community. These are not typically people in the business of developing, and they often do this as a one-shot deal to raise some cash. These resident landowners may be more sensitive and responsive to concerns raised by neighbors, so a less contentious approach might succeed.

For the most part, developers come into a community, buy and resell land as fast as possible, and exit the community, profit in hand. Developers do not care about the long-term interests of the community, except as the consequences may affect their reputation, pocketbook, or ability to make money in the future.

I am so often amazed at the partnership of local officials and developers. Perhaps it is the siren of tax revenues that seduces local officials. However, I rarely see the calculation of revenues being offset by realistic estimates of the costs and expenses of development. Simply look at any growing community and ask whether the taxes are going down. It is unlikely.

General principles for dealing with developers

Depending upon the attitude and sophistication of your local government, it may be open to suggestions about how to deal with developers. In my own experience, local government has not always been receptive to citizen input. However, some good results are possible: (a) Government might actually take some or all of your suggestions; (b) Even if government does not use your suggestions in the near term, some of these ideas may be considered and incorporated in the future; (c) Your suggestions will cast doubt on both the credibility of the developer and on the decision-making process of government, and may serve to build grassroots support for your position.

More so now than ten years ago, government is increasingly viewing its relationship with developers as a business negotiation. Many jurisdictions provide for developer agreements, in which a developer makes legal commitments as to funding and other aspects of a development in return for support by local government in the form of annexation, tax incentives, wastewater treatment, or other incentives or considerations. You should insist on a developer agreement. Depending on the experience of your government, it may be negotiating a major development for the first time, facing a developer who is in the business of doing this. A development will permanently affect your community's finances and quality of life; a carefully written developer agreement can protect your community.

For all these reasons, you may wish to advocate some or all of these suggestions to your government:

1. *Accept help from qualified, impartial experts.* Has your community gone through a development planning process? Have you identified such factors as (a) the capacity and costs of existing public facilities and services; (b) service standards for the entire community, and existing deficiencies; (c) methods for assigning the proportionate share of municipal costs to new development; and (d) the effect of development on the existing tax structure? It is fair to ask a developer to split the cost of such planning expertise. The developer will not want to do that, because of the cost and time involved, and because much of this planning may reflect negatively on the proposed development. But ask him and make him say "no" publicly.

2. *Accept help from citizens.* Government will rely on all manner of expertise from a developer, but frequently will not accept help from its own citizens. Nonetheless, you should offer. It would be good for your cause to have a "place at the table" to influence decision making from within. Don't count on it, however.

3. *Don't rely on answers from the developer.* Asking a developer to answer your community's planning concerns is a little like asking the fox to comment on chicken-coop security. A developer has strong interests that do not coincide with the community's interests.

4. *Keep the developer at arm's length during negotiations.* Many communities do not approach a development decision as an arm's-length business negotiation. Your government officials must be made to realize that each side has its own interests. Your elected officials should strongly represent the interests of your community. In the best of circumstances, you may negotiate a developer's agreement, which is an actual legal contract between

the developer and the local government. During this and any process, the developer will represent only his own interests. It is naive at best and destructive at worst to imagine that a developer will represent the interests of your community.

5. *Don't give away your crown jewel.* If the developer needs something from your government, don't give it without getting something in return. For Fischer Creek, the crown jewel of the village was annexation. Yet the village board never figured out that once they granted the annexation, they lost all their negotiating power. Once the developer has annexed his land, he does not need anything else from the village by way of concessions. People forget that developers are not legally entitled to annexation or a zoning change. A government should extract benefits from the developer in exchange for any cooperation that government is not legally required to provide.

6. *Take the time to understand the issues.* Haste usually benefits the developer. It rarely benefits the community. The community has many more issues to think about than does the developer. The developer deals with the profit of a one-time transaction; local government has to project how the development will affect the community economically, socially, and environmentally over many years to come. Although things may initially seem clear or simple, once you slow things down, many questions and issues will surface. Give yourself the opportunity to gather information relevant to these issues.

7. *Actively set the agenda.* The developer will steer debate toward issues that benefit his agenda. He may want to focus on engineering issues (which always get solved and carry with them the assumption that the development is going forward). You may want to focus on planning issues, site suitability, taxation, and effects. Don't let the developer define the terms of the debate.

Are the concessions real?

Even if a developer appears to make concessions, determine whether the concessions are real or are mere window dressing. For Fischer Creek, the developer came forward with "concessions" in the form of setting aside fifty acres of the parcel for conservation. Upon examination of the revised plat, we concluded that the developer took his required setbacks from the lake and creek, along with areas needed for storm water runoff, and packaged them as a "concession." This was land he already had to leave vacant for legal or engineering reasons. Sometimes, developers will propose higher density than they need or think they can get, knowing that density will be reduced and it will then appear that they made a "concession" on that as well.

As debate on Fischer Creek continued, the developer began to pick up the language of the opposition. He talked about "open space" and "green space," terms completely absent from his initial presentations. Unfortunately, the developer was referring to lawns, but his mere use of the lingo helped his public image initially. He had the audacity to refer to his proposal as "the most environmentally sensitive development in the state," even though he didn't hire a landscape architect until months after making his initial proposal and had no idea about the ecological features of the site he proposed to destroy. Essentially, he proposed superimposing a suburban subdivision on an environmentally sensitive area, with no conservation design considerations for the site. When he finally hired a landscape architect, who proposed some cosmetic changes, he tried to sell this as a major concession as well.

How developers operate

As a general matter, you can expect some or all of the following tactics from a developer:

1. *Bluster.* Talk is cheap. Maybe that's why developers do so much of it. A developer may tell you how it's always done, or how it's never done, or how much he's done. Take it all with a grain of salt. The developer in Fischer Creek went on the record several times stating that the site would never be a park. Despite information that state and county officials were seeking to buy the property for a park, he said, "No one is coming down the pike to buy it for a park. Not in these days when government doesn't have money enough for schools and other things." About a month later, he reiterated, "It's not a park site, it's not a public site, and it's not going

to be." He also stated, "We totally control this property." Developers act with a lot of confidence and aggression. Don't be fooled or intimidated by the bluster.

2. *Bully.* Developers will bully you if you let them. Like the school-yard bully of grade-school days, developers prey on you if they sense weakness. In Fischer Creek, the developers demanded that no one discuss the land except them and threatened a SLAPP suit. That was a pathetic attempt to intimidate the Friends around the time that momentum was building for our position. In a neighboring township, a developer threatened litigation as a device to quiet the town chairman and win approval of a site design inconsistent with the town's land-use plan. The developer and local officials both used name-calling and threats to get us to back off. For Hika Conservancy, one of the developers used personal attacks to try to undermine the opposition. He went after John Kirsch, one of the board members supporting conservancy, and said that John had a conflict of interest because he lived across the street from the site. He tried to get John to recuse himself at village board meetings so that he could not vote AND could not participate in any debate. Luckily, John (who has unblemished integrity), the village board, and community members rallied, and the attack may ultimately have done the developer more harm than good.

3. *Bluff.* Some developers can say anything with a straight face. Call it bluffing or call it an outright lie, the effect is the same. For Fischer Creek, the developer threatened to do the development in the town if the village refused annexation. That was a bluff because the lower density in the town could not support the land cost. After Cleveland defeated the annexation, it was just a few weeks before the developers turned tail and left. For Hika Conservancy, the developers claimed that the Kohler Company had expressed interest in putting a hotel on the site. Their tactic, which may have worked briefly, was to get the board to think of a condominium development as the "lesser" of two evils and so approve it. We knew, simply by looking at land cost and the square footage cost of building a motel, that the developer's statement was nonsense. The return on investment wasn't there. To reinforce our

conclusion with facts, someone called the Kohler Company and spoke to the head of their hospitality division. That senior corporate officer agreed to be quoted at the village board meeting as saying that the Kohler Company was not considering the Cleveland site. On that one, I decided to call the developer's bluff, and strongly supported having a hotel on the site. I gave many reasons why that would be better than multifamily development and said I would support it fully, under certain conditions. For Point Creek, the landowner also tried a bluff, stating that he had an offer on the property for $1.8 million. We knew that was nonsense, because if he had had the offer in hand he would have taken it. His only interest was money, and he didn't care whose it was. There is no way he would have turned down $1.8 million cash out of deference to our efforts. Perhaps someone on your team plays poker. Put that person in charge of negotiation strategy.

If the developer is attacking, threatening, and bullying, it may be a sign that you are being effective. The more effective you are, the stronger the retaliation from the developer. Try not to be discouraged if the developer is lashing out. The developer may try to split the community so that citizens will fight with each other instead of against the developer. Stay on course and keep doing what you have been doing. It is probably going to be successful, or the developer would not feel so threatened and desperate.

Raise every question you can imagine.

Sometimes it is enough to raise questions. You don't need all the answers. By raising questions, you can identify concerns from a broad range of citizens and build support by finding allies across a range of issues. Also, local officials may begin to realize they are making a decision with insufficient information. Rather than look ignorant or stupid, government officials may be more comfortable doing nothing. Governments are great at doing nothing. If "no action" is your strategic goal, it should not be that hard to figure out a way to get government not to do anything.

The following are the kinds of questions you can raise to get more information and/or to slow down the project:

1. How will the proposed development affect the tax base?
    a. How much property-tax revenue will be generated?
    b. When will you see that revenue?
    c. What are the short-term and long-term expenses? What are the contingent expenses?
    d. How will the development affect current property assessments?
    e. Will taxes still go up because of higher assessments?
    f. Will higher taxes affect the ability of people on fixed incomes to stay in their homes and in the community?
    g. What will happen to school taxes?
    h. Is the developer willing to pay a fee to offset loss of revenue?
2. How will the proposed development affect utility costs?
    a. How much capacity will the proposed development use?
    b. What is the value of that capacity?
    c. Is the developer willing to compensate for the value of that capacity?
3. What has been the experience of other communities that have had similar developments?
    a. What are the names of similar developments?
    b. What has been the experience of the surrounding communities?
    c. What were the short-term and long-term costs?
    d. What would those communities do differently now?
    e. Did development affect the quality of life in the community?
    f. Did the community remain intact?
    g. How do people in that community feel about the development?
4. What will be the effect of the increased traffic?
    a. Will roads suffer more wear?
    b. Will traffic pose a safety hazard?
    c. What traffic patterns will be used?
    d. Will we need more police to control speeding?
    e. How will the increased noise, traffic, and pollution affect the quality of life?

5. What is the environmental impact of the proposed development?
   a. What is the ecological significance of the site?
   b. Is it unique or unusual in any respects?
   c. How will all the habitats of the area be affected?
   d. Is there a current environmental impact assessment?
   e. If so, why haven't we seen it?
   f. If not, should we require one?
   g. Should we require setbacks that allow wildlife to be undisturbed in their breeding, shelter, and feeding patterns?
   h. Should we designate a green-space or conservancy area?
   i. Should we provide for environmental corridors?
   j. Is there area set aside for trails?
6. What is the historical significance of the area?
   a. What archaeological interest does the site have?
   b. What Native American interest does the site have?
   c. What is the local and cultural history of the site?
7. What are all the short-term and long-term costs?
   a. Have we identified all utilities and services to be provided?
   b. Have we projected these costs for three-, five-, and ten-year periods?
   c. What kinds of services will the new residents expect?
   d. Will they expect services that we do not presently provide?
   e. If there are costs, do we want to negotiate a developer's agreement?
8. Will the development bring any other economic benefits to the area?
   a. Will it bring additional customers to existing businesses?
   b. Will it help establish new businesses?
   c. Are we maximizing the economic benefit from development of this site?

Sample responses to the developer

Although the facts and ordinances in each land battle are different, many of the issues are similar, as are developer's responses to those issues. Here are some sample responses to issues that you may be addressing with a developer.

Developer: Anticipated tax revenue will be [zillions of] dollars.

Response: Developer calculates tax revenues based on certain assumptions, such as that all homes are built and occupied and assessed at the value he gives. Also, there may be complicated tax calculations in your state as there are in Wisconsin. Because we have "revenue share," the Village receives only 60 cents per dollar of tax revenue, so any figure would be immediately reduced for that and perhaps other reasons.

Developer: There are no short-term expenses and long-term expenses are minimal.

Response: The Urban Land Institute and other planning organizations publish lengthy books on how to quantify the impacts of development, including software for calculating the financial costs of development.

Developer: You will have more net revenues.

Response: Most sophisticated studies now show that almost invariably, with residential development, expenses rise to meet or exceed the increased revenue.

Developer: The development will have no effect on the ability of people on fixed incomes to stay in their homes.

Response: There are two issues here. First, will taxes in fact go up because expenses will exceed revenues? Second is the issue of assessed value. Even if taxes do not go up, if the development raises assessed value, people will pay more taxes. A rise in assessed value benefits people when they sell their homes, but results in more taxes when people want to stay in their homes. Thus, a project which raises assessed value can be a community-buster.

Developer: The development will not result in higher taxes. Therefore, it is unnecessary to discuss whether we will reimburse the community for any costs.

Response: The developer should "put his money where his mouth is." If he is confident in his calculations, he should be willing to make up any shortfalls if his calculations are deficient and local government relied on them.

Developer: Increase in traffic volume will have no adverse effect on the roads.
Response: Planning sources indicate that increased traffic volume has numerous effects, such as requiring increased police patrols, causing additional road wear, affecting safety, increasing commuting times, and compromising quality of life (by increasing noise, pollution, etc.).

Developer: The development will have no adverse impact on the ecology of the site. Only a small portion of the landscape will actually be altered.
Response: The developer fails to address basic principles of conservation biology, such as edge effects, habitat fragmentation, and endemic populations. The physical changes do and will dramatically affect the entire ecosystem of areas beyond the bounds of the proposed development.

Developer: The habitat of the area will be slightly altered to the extent that roads and homes will be constructed. Wildlife adapts to change.
Response: The habitat will be dramatically altered. The property will go from a semi-wild, undeveloped state to one that is fragmented and less ecologically stable. "Wildlife adapts to change" is a completely inaccurate statement when we speak in terms of biological diversity and species abundance and diversity. In other words, measuring the success of adaptive animals like raccoons does not take into account potential rare or threatened species whose habitat requirements are more tightly defined and more sensitive to environmental perturbations.

Do the best you can.

Dealing with a developer or landowner may be the most challenging and frustrating part of your land battle. You may be faced with someone who has totally different values and priorities. You may be faced with someone with much more experience and resources. You may be forced to accede to a vision valuing money over all other values and live in that world for a time, especially if your energies are devoted to raising the purchase price for the land, that is, finding a big pile of money for a developer. However, the odds are the developer or landowner is not smarter than you. And probably does not have your commitment or long-term staying power for the cause. The developer probably does not have a coalition behind him. And may not have your flexibility, maneuverability, and moxie. Go get 'em!

CHAPTER TEN

MANAGING THE PROCESS

(Roller-coaster Ride)

Land battles are stressful.

If you are contemplating a land battle, be realistic. It will be stressful. If you are already involved in a land battle, you know this to be true. You are putting yourself and your beliefs on the line. That's hard. What is even harder is the fact that your fortunes rest largely on matters outside your personal control. To care so much but control so little—that's stressful.

It is also stressful to engage in activities that you do not like or do not do well. It is even more stressful when something you care passionately about rests on your success at these activities.

In most land battles, you will face a "do-or-die" situation. Missing a deadline for payment, losing a crucial vote, being denied a grant. Any of these outcomes could mean your efforts fail. More often, of the defeats and victories along the way, none is a final disposition, so you have to keep fighting. You need stamina and commitment to keep going. Celebrate your victories. They will buoy you and propel you forward. There will be far more times of frustration, so cherish your wins when you get them.

The ups and downs of a land battle

In both Fischer Creek and Point Creek, we had numerous ups and downs. Knowing about them will give you an idea of what to expect, so you can be as prepared as possible. Also, they provide a message of hope. Even after the low points, we kept going and ultimately prevailed.

The following is a summary of the highs and lows of Point Creek:

- We learn a housing development is planned for the Point Creek Watershed. (low)
- County committee tables the developer's variance request for a long cul-de-sac, which the developer needs in order to develop the property. (high)
- County committee ultimately approves the variance request at a subsequent hearing. (low)
- Landowner is willing to talk to our group about purchase of the land and comes from Colorado to meet with us in Wisconsin. (high)
- Landowner is inflexible on $1.9 million asking price. (low)
- We learn state stewardship fund is interested in the parcel. State could fund 50 percent of the appraised value of the parcel. (high)
- We are awarded $250,000 grant from West Foundation. (high)
- We learn West Foundation grant is two-for-one matching grant, so we have to raise another $500,000 in private funds in order to get their $250,000. (low)
- We are almost $250,000 short on the match a couple of weeks before West Foundation deadline. (low)
- Just before Christmas, we receive a $200,000 anonymous donation. (high)
- West Foundation extends our deadline by three months. (high)
- Our key fund-raiser is diagnosed with cancer. (low)
- We meet the West Foundation challenge grant. (high)
- Appraised value for the parcel comes in at $1.3 million. Even if we get the 50 percent grant from the state DNR stewardship fund, we are still almost $500,000 short. (low)
- Landowner refuses to budge from his price or work with us on structuring the transaction using tax incentives or other means. (low)
- We learn of a one-time federal grant making $6.5 million available to the Wisconsin Coastal Management Program for land purchases along the Great Lakes, at a 75 percent match. (high)
- We are ranked number one in the state for the stewardship fund application. (high)

- Our lawyer, in charge of negotiating with the landowner, is diagnosed with cancer. (low)
- The Wisconsin Coastal Management program indicates we are highly ranked for their grant award. (high)
- The Wisconsin Coastal Management program informs us that in order to stay in competition for their grant, we must have a signed deal with the landowner within ten days. (low)
- Our lawyer recovers from cancer and says he can get the agreement done in one week. (high)
- Wisconsin Coastal Management grant is awarded for $800,000. (high)
- Stewardship grant of $600,000 receives objections in state legislature. (low)
- Massive lobbying campaign is mounted to dislodge stewardship funds from state legislature in Madison. (low)
- Landowner refuses to extend closing date on purchase agreement while we attempt to dislodge funds. (low)
- Two days before the landowner's deadline, state legislature releases funds. (high)
- In final review process before issuing stewardship fund check for $600,000, state DNR auditors have questions about site cleanup, and move to delay issuing check. (low)
- The state DNR check is already in the mail and the escrow closes for purchase of Point Creek. (high)

As you can see, for Point Creek most of the highs and lows had to do with whether we could raise enough money within the developer's deadline. When you can so clearly see the benefits of conservation, it is difficult and stressful to spend most of your energy on groveling for money. You wish the landowner could see and share at least some of your land ethic.

The history of Fischer Creek was different, with many of the events being political, but there were even more highs and lows in that scenario:

- We learn that a Chicago developer wants to build a 150-unit planned development in the Fischer Creek Watershed, a mile north of my cottage on Lake Michigan. Developer requests annexation of the land to Village of Cleveland so he can take advantage of municipal sewer and water and higher density permitted in village zoning ordinances. (low)

- Neighbors have first meeting and want to fight the development. Diverse group includes array of educated, highly motivated citizens. Group quickly organizes to form Friends of Fischer Creek. (high)
- Village president, chairman of plan commission, and majority of the members of both the plan commission and the village board appear to support the development. (low)
- We learn that to defeat annexation, we do not need a majority of the village board; we need only three "no" votes from among seven members. (high)
- Two outspoken members of the plan commission advocate the need for getting more information and slowing the process. (high)
- Chairman of Town of Centerville says the town will challenge annexation. (high)
- Friends of Fischer Creek hold their first public meeting and more than a hundred citizens and members of the media attend. (high)
- State Department of Administration approves petition for annexation as being in the public interest, even though it notes that the plat is unacceptable for the land configuration. (low)
- Local paper runs editorial recommending that the village delay action on annexation and get more information. (high)
- Friends get approximately two hundred signatures from village residents on a petition asking for annexation to be delayed six months so that the village can engage in further fact finding on the consequences of development. (high)
- Village board ignores petition. (low)
- County officials tell Friends that the actual chance of buying Fischer Creek for a park is quite low. (low)
- Jeff Pagels, of the state DNR, appears at plan commission meeting and discusses the process for the state's buying the Fischer Creek land for a park. (high)
- As Friends of Fischer Creek gain support, village officials lash out and tell me to "go back where you came from." (low)
- Dr. Jack Huddleston comes to Cleveland from Madison, Wiscon-

sin, and hosts a seminar for village officials on visioning, planning for growth, and the impacts of major development. (high)

- Several village board members leave Huddleston seminar believing he favored annexation and development at Fischer Creek. (low)
- Friends distribute green "Save Fischer Creek" signs, and signs begin appearing in windows throughout the community. (high)
- Developer sends threatening letter demanding that the Friends cease communications concerning Fischer Creek and threatening legal action if we do not comply. (low)
- Local paper prints editorial condemning developer for his strong-arm tactics against the Friends of Fischer Creek. (high)
- Friends hold their second public meeting and distribute a land-use plan written by them showing Fischer Creek as a park and identifying many other areas within the Village of Cleveland that could be used for development. (high)
- Friends commence a referendum campaign on the issue of annexation. We need sixty-five signatures on the petition to meet the legal requirements to put the referendum on the ballot, and we get 348 signatures. (high)
- Village board rejects annexation when three village board members vote "no." Developer and village president are stunned. (high)
- Friends learn that the developer can file a second petition for annexation in 120 days, starting the whole process over. (low)
- Developer pulls out, terminating his interest in the development in both the Village of Cleveland (with annexation) and in the Town of Centerville. (high)
- In the April election, Friends run our own slate of candidates for village trustee and village president. (high)
- County sheriff removes many of the Friends' lawn signs for candidates in politically motivated enforcement action. (low)
- In a major public outcry over sheriff's actions, irate citizens meet with sheriff at county seat, and signs are returned and replaced on lawns. (high)
- The property of various members of Friends is vandalized. (low)
- Friends win village president and two out of three trustee positions. (high)

- Referendum preventing annexation of Fischer Creek loses by a small margin. (low)
- One of the Friends' candidates for office is forced to resign from the village board because of threats made to his employer by the village. (low)
- Village board elects a pro-development Trustee to replace Friends candidate who is forced to resign. (low)
- First three appraisals for state DNR stewardship grant are all far below the seller's asking price for Fischer Creek. (low)
- State DNR helps Friends find two more appraisers with expertise in Lake Michigan shoreline appraisals. (high)
- State makes available $1 million toward purchase of Fischer Creek. (high)
- County finds $300,000 to make up rest of purchase price and agrees to manage the property for the state. (high)
- At the DNR meeting to vote on the acquisition, a representative of the governor indicates we will get his signature only if the southern part of the parcel is sold off for development. (low)
- Governor signs off on acquisition, and (most of) Fischer Creek is saved in perpetuity. (high)
- The state bureaucracy grinds slowly, and the sale of subdivided lots adjoining Fischer Creek is delayed for approximately five years. (high)
- Governor demands that Fischer Creek lots finally be sold. (low)
- Village of Cleveland, under changed leadership, has its village engineer determine that the lots are not buildable because there is insufficient setback from the high bluff. The village indicates that it will refuse to issue building permits on the site. (high)
- Lake frontage lots adjoining southernmost part of Fischer Creek Park are formally added to the park. (high)

Tips for handling the stress of land battles

Everybody has his or her own methods for battling stress. I marshal my internal resources and seek support from others. The important thing is to know yourself. Do what you need to do to survive. Here are some tips for handling the stress of land battles:

1. *Make sure you have a team of people who can share the burden and share the work.* During Fischer Creek, we rotated who carried the load, so that team members could rest and focus on other things in their lives. We did not do this formally. It just happened that people were there to step in and handle matters when needed. As it turns out, a rotating leadership group is often key to successful grassroots activism. We "lucked" into it in the past, but in the future, I would try my best to make sure it's there.

2. *Try to maintain some balance in your life.* When things get overwhelming, step back and enjoy activities that relax and energize you. For me, it was walking, writing, cross country skiing, yoga, gardening, golf, and music. For others it may be chopping wood, coaching soccer, hunting, cooking, camping, fishing, running, hiking, painting—whatever. Try to touch base with your normal life and keep some perspective on the role of the land battle in your life.

3. *Stay focused on your strategic goal.* Try not to be distracted by extraneous events that may not have much to do with the important issues. There is a great tendency to react to every rumor, event, or piece of information. A lot of it is not true, and still more of it may not affect your strategy. Use your energy toward your strategic goals; avoid the temptation to get involved in and react to everything that's going on.

4. *Interact with people who will energize, praise, and support you.* Get the benefits of being part of a team of like-minded people working on a common goal. Benefit from the support of friends and family. Avoid "naysayers."

5. *Be prepared to compromise.* Be flexible. You may be able to recast seeming defeat into victory. Perhaps you could not save the parcel for a nature conservancy but were able to reduce density from thirty-six units to six; perhaps you do not have full public access to the land, but negotiated beach and fishing rights. Feel proud of what you did accomplish against all odds. Focus on the victory, not the loss.

6. *Never give up.* Early on in Fischer Creek, Rolf gave me a picture, captioned, "Never give up," of a big bird being strangled by a frog it had swallowed. I posted that cartoon in my study for years.

Sometimes, Providence may step in to help you. You have to keep the issue alive so that Providence can do its thing.

7. *Return to the site you are trying to preserve.* Let nature work its magic on your spirit. Remember why you are doing all this.

During our fight for Point Creek, while we were madly scrambling to find the unfathomable sum of $1.9 million, Rolf and I made a trip to the State Department of Natural Resources in Green Bay. On the way home, we chose a route that took us over Point Creek and past the site. It was the middle of the day, a time when the birds and critters are usually hidden. But as we slowed down to traverse the bridge over Point Creek, a huge great blue heron stood in the creek right next to the road and watched us go by. That encounter—make of it what you will—kept me going for many long months thereafter.

Keep fighting the good fight. The universe will thank you.

Index

academics. *See* universities
aerial photos and maps, 115, 129
American Club (Kohler, WI), 105
annexation, 20, 24, 25, 56, 141; in
  the Fischer Creek land battle, 5, 7,
  26, 45–49, 62–63, 92–98, 100–101,
  140, 143, 145, 154–157; in the Hika
  Conservancy land battle, 112
attorneys. *See* lawyers
Audobon Society, 81

bald eagle, 12
Baumgart, Jim, 119
Big Brothers Big Sisters, 85
Biological Inventory of Kingfisher
  Farm, 40, 128
Boy Scouts, 74–75

Centerville, Town of: and dairy
  farming, 89; and the Fischer Creek
  land battle, 3, 5, 82, 99, 155, 156;
  land-use plan of, with Cleveland, 7, 39, 46, 73, 102, 127; and
  the Point Creek land battle, 38;
  and procedures for variances on
  zoning, 87
Centerville Creek, 12
chamber of commerce, 136
Chicago, 3, 4, 13, 126, 154; developers, 7, 30; lawyers, 23, 28, 63
Class 1 trout streams, 4, 49

Cleveland, Village of, 2, 21, 27, 63,
  64, 99, 128, 157: aerial photos of,
  115; disseminating information
  in, 74–75; in Fischer Creek land
  battle, 3, 5, 22, 45–46, 101–102,
  145; in the Hika Conservancy land
  battle, 12–14, 43, 66, 121; joint
  land-use plan of, with Centerville,
  7, 39, 46, 73, 95–96, 102, 127; and
  the media, 103, 109; and the Point
  Creek land battle, 128; quality of
  life in, 50, 83, 92–93, 96–97; referendum about, wording of, 51;
  and "revenue share," 149; traffic
  in, 105; wastewater treatment in,
  29, 92, 93; zoning in, 24, 86–87
Cleveland Neighborhood Plan, 102
Cleveland Plan Commission: in
  Fischer Creek land battle, 3–5, 27,
  34, 47, 49–50, 62, 64, 83, 94, 97–
  98, 155; in Hika Conservancy land
  battle, 44, 66, 74
Cleveland Village Board: in Fischer
  Creek land battle, 46, 49–50, 63,
  64, 83, 143, 155, 157; in Hika Conservancy land battle, 44, 66, 67,
  74, 145–146
cluster development, 28
coalition building, 15, 16, 69–85
Coastal grant. *See* Wisconsin
  Coastal Management Program

Cofrin Center for Biodiversity, 84
colleges. *See* universities
conditional use, 20, 21, 23, 24, 86
conservation biology, 82, 150
conservation easements, 8, 84, 108, 123
conservation organizations, 15, 27, 60, 79–81, 84. *See also individual organizations*
counsel, legal. *See* lawyers

dairy farming, 3, 10, 89–90
Data Compilation and Assessment of Coastal Wetlands of Wisconsin's Great Lakes, 39, 127–128
Defined Environmental Corridors Map, 128
delay, strategy of, 48, 49, 73, 112, 140, 146–148
Democratic party, 110
Demske, Mike, 89–90, 122, 126, 133
Department of Natural Resources (DNR). *See* Wisconsin Department of Natural Resources
developers, 15, 18, 72, 88–89; in the Fischer Creek land battle, 49, 63, 73, 98–99, 103, 105; opposing, 138–151; and the press, 104, 112
disinformation, 40–41
DNR. *See* Wisconsin Department of Natural Resources
Ducks Unlimited, 81

editorials, 106, 112–113, 136, 155, 156. *See also* media
elections, 100–101, 117–118, 156. *See also* referendums
e-mail, use of in land battles, 36–37, 114
environment: effects of development on, 22, 28, 93, 148, 150
environmental impact studies, 24, 140, 148

environmentally sensitive developments, 28, 144
environmental organizations. *See* conservation organizations

Falk, Kathleen, 27
farmland, 24, 89–90
Fischer Creek Alliance, 72, 128
Fischer Creek Conservation Area, 7
Fischer Creek land battle, 2, 3–7, 9, 22, 36, 69, 72, 99, 128; contributions of supporters in, 75; election campaign during, 100–101; fund-raising in, 78, 116, 117, 118, 123–124, 125; highs and lows of, 154–157; use of history in, 30; identifying issues in, 26–27; influence of, on Point Creek acquisition, 127; information presented during, 92–98; leadership circle for, 32, 33–34, 41–42, 125; legal counsel in, 59–60, 62–65, 91, 98; materials related to, 74–75; and the media, 17, 78, 91, 103–109, 111–113; motivation behind, 34–35; opposing the developer in, 138, 139, 140, 143, 144–146; people consulted during, 27–30; public meetings during, 77; and Rolf Johnson, 32, 41, 47, 97–98, 99; strategy in, 45–51, 53. *See also* Friends of Fischer Creek
501(c)(3) entity, 84, 118, 120, 121
Fogelson, Gerald, 4, 5, 35
Fond du Lac County, Wisconsin, 8
Friends of Fischer Creek, 8, 11, 81, 91, 101; beginnings of, 6, 155; checking account for, 117; community vision of, 95–96; and counsel, 62–65; credibility of, 47; leaflets for, 75; logo of, 72–73, 78; and the media, 104, 112, 156; name of, 71

Friis, Mike, 124–125
fund-raising, 15, 17–18, 89, 114–137;
in Fischer Creek land battle, 46,
47, 48, 78, 83; in Point Creek land
battle, 10–12, 38, 40, 51–52, 65,
69, 71–72; by tapping into the
land-trust community, 84
Furmanski, Julie, 48

Girl Scouts, 74
grants and grant writing, 15, 18,
79, 119, 137; private foundation,
106, 110, 134–135; public (government), 90, 110–111, 123–134, 153,
154
grassroots activism, 14, 16, 46;
and disinformation, 40; in the
Hika Convervancy land battle,
99–100; leadership of, 158; in
the Point Creek land battle, 82;
uncontrollability of, 47
great blue herons, 1, 9, 12, 40, 73,
74, 159
Great Lakes: and conservation
efforts, 107; property along, 39;
Watershed, 8
Great Lakes United, 80
Green Bay, Wisconsin, 27, 49, 107,
126, 159
"green space." See "open space"

habitat: effects of development on,
15, 26, 35, 47, 81, 89, 148, 150; for
great blue heron, 9; for lake trout,
4, 27, 49; for salmon, 4. See also
wildlife
Heuel, Robert, 78
Hika Conservancy land battle, 2, 12–
14, 71; avoidance of the media
during, 99–100, 108–109; and citizen activism, 91; and Cleveland
land-use plan, 102; community
support for, 70; fund-raising in,

118, 121; legal counsel in, 57, 65–
68, 91, 98; materials related to, 74;
opposing the developer in, 138,
139, 145; strategy in, 52–53, 100;
and the Wimpffens, 42–44, 116
Hika Cove, 5, 6, 112
Hika Park, 12, 14, 42, 44, 65
Huddleston, Dr. Jack, 27, 82–83,
96–97, 99, 155–156
Huhn, Cindy, 91
hunting organizations, 81

Internet, 114; Web site for Wisconsin
DNR, 128

Johnson, Rolf: and the Fischer
Creek land battle, 32, 47, 72, 97,
99, 115, 158; and the media, 104,
107, 108; and the Point Creek land
battle, 8, 9, 80, 129, 135
Joint Finance Committee. See
Wisconsin State Legislature
Joint Land Use Plan (of the Town
of Centerville and the Village of
Cleveland), 7, 39, 46, 102, 127
Joint Plan Commission (of the Town
of Centerville and the Village of
Cleveland), 7–8

Kaiser, Kurt, 101
Kingfisher Farm, 39–40, 128
Kirchener, Jerry, 81
Kirsch, Idell, 36, 101
Kirsch, John, 32, 36, 41–42, 47, 48,
101, 102, 116, 117, 145
Kiwanis club, 80
Knowles-Newlson Stewardship Pro-
gram. See Stewardship Program
(Wisconsin Department of Natural
Resources)
Kohler, Wisconsin, 105. See also
American Club
Kohler Company, 145–146

Lake Michigan, 2, 3, 4, 7, 9, 106; beach, in the Hika Conservancy, 12; development along, 22, 24, 35, 65, 126; and migratory birds, 9; shoreline, appraisals of, 157; shoreline, from the air, 115; shoreline, protection of, 89, 102; wetlands, 128

Lake Michigan Federation, 80

Lake Michigan Watershed, 9, 80

land battles. *See* Fischer Creek land battle; Hika Conservancy land battle; Point Creek land battle

land conservancy (or land trust), 84, 89, 120. *See also* Sheboygan Area Land Conservancy

Land Legacy Study. *See* Wisconsin Department of Natural Resources

landscape architects, 28, 144

land-use ordinances, 15, 66, 82

land-use plans, 7-8, 43, 46, 86, 87, 95-96, 101-102, 145, 156

Langdon, Jim, 124-125

lawsuits. *See* litigation

lawyers, 15, 16, 23-24, 29, 55-68, 114; and delay strategy, 48, 49; hiring, 33; paying for, 60-62, 67-68, 98, 115-116; use of, in Fischer Creek land battle, 59-60, 61-65, 91; use of, in Hika Conservancy land battle, 65-68; use of, in Point Creek land battle, 65, 132; working pro bono, 60, 61, 65. *See also* litigation

leadership circle, in land battles, 32, 41-42, 76-77, 79, 114, 117, 125

Lee, Stan, 11

letters to the editor, 33, 106. *See also* media

Lions club, 80

litigation, 57-58, 99, 145. *See also* lawyers

lobbying, 70, 83, 111, 118-120, 133, 136, 154

local government, 15, 17, 76; and budget cuts, 111; dealing with, with help from lawyers, 56; and developers, 138, 141-143; and elections, 100-101; influencing, 86-102; meetings, 3-4; sensitivities of people in, 98

local unit of government (LUG), 83, 88-100, 121, 122, 128

logging, 90

logos, 72-74

LUG. *See* local unit of government

Madison, Wisconsin, 27, 136, 155; lobbying in, 11, 65, 70, 133, 154. *See also* Wisconsin State Legislature

Manitowoc (city in Wisconsin), 3, 72, 106, 128; Chamber of Commerce of, 107; newspaper of, 84; radio show of, 107

Manitowoc County, Wisconsin, 7, 8, 9, 63, 81, 87; cooperation of, in Point Creek land battle, 72, 89-90, 122-123; and West Foundation, 10, 69, 134; wetlands of, 39, 127

Manitowoc County Board, 113

Manitowoc County Defined Environmental Corridors Map, 128

Manitowoc County Park and Open Space Plan, 128

Manitowoc County Planning and Parks Commission, 81, 90, 122, 128

Manitowoc County Planning Department, 115

Manitowoc Herald, 112

Mayer, Peter, 11, 13, 63, 66-67

Maywood Environmental Center (Sheboygan), 81

McCallum, Scott (governor of Wisconsin), 11, 132
media, 15, 17, 33, 71, 72, 82, 88, 95–96; campaign, conducting, 103–113; in Fischer Creek land battle, 48, 77, 91, 95–96, 99, 116; in Hika Conservancy land battle, 99–100; lack of, in Cleveland, 74; in Point Creek land battle, 84. *See also* newspapers; radio; television
migratory birds and animals, 9, 12. *See also* great blue heron
Milwaukee, 3, 4, 65, 125
Milwaukee Public Museum, 107
"Morning Show," 107

National Oceanic and Atmospheric Administration (NOAA), 119, 122
Native Americans, 30, 148
Nature Conservancy, the, 81, 119
newspapers, 105–106, 112–113, 155. *See also* editorials; letters to the editor; *Manitowoc Herald; Sheboygan Press*

open-meetings statute, 56, 57
"open space," 15, 89, 91, 128, 144, 148

Pagels, Jeff, 27, 49, 97–98, 124, 129, 130, 155
parks and planning department. *See* Manitowoc County Planning and Parks Commission
partnerships. *See* coalition building
PERC. *See* Public Environmental Resource Center
petitions, use of in land battles, 27, 33, 48, 56, 75, 155
Pirrung, Don, 42, 50
plan commissions, 57, 86, 87, 88, 139. *See also* Cleveland Plan Commission

Point Creek land battle, 2, 7–12, 18, 22, 90, 128; e-mail, use of during, 36; fund-raising in, 69, 89, 118, 121–122, 123, 124, 126–136; group logo, use of, 74; group name, importance of, 71–72; highs and lows of, 153–154; legal bills during, 116; materials related to, 38–40, 73–74; and the media, 104, 106, 107, 109, 110, 111; opposing the developer in, 138, 139; partnerships in, 80, 82–84; strategy in, 51–52
Point Creek Natural Area, 11, 12
Point Creek Watershed Initiative, 127
pollution, 49, 147, 150
pro-bono cases. *See* lawyers
Public Environmental Resource Center (PERC), 78
publicity. *See* media

quality of life, 26, 47, 50, 95, 147

radio, 106–107, 116. *See also* media
referendums, use of in land battles, 42, 50, 64, 74, 100–101, 112, 156, 157
Republican party, 110, 111
revenue sharing, 96, 149
right of protest, 24, 53, 67
River Protection Grant, 128
Rotary Club, 80

SALC. *See* Sheboygan Area Land Conservancy
Schaper, Ron, 40, 133
Schmitz, Gary, 4, 5, 64
septic systems, 126. *See also* sewage and water services; wastewater treatment
setbacks, 16, 20, 24, 87, 148; in developer's agreement, 93; DNR information about, 27; in Fischer

Creek land battle, 144, 157; in Point Creek land battle, 22, 38–39, 51

sewer and water services, 5, 22, 26. *See also* septic systems; wastewater treatment

Sheboygan (city in Wisconsin), 3, 8, 71–72, 81, 106

Sheboygan Area Land Conservancy (SALC): and fund-raising, 83, 120, 121–122, 125, 128, 134–135; and legal counsel, 116; motivation behind forming, 8; name of, 71–72

Sheboygan County, Wisconsin, 8

Sheboygan Marina, 105

Sheboygan Press, 64, 78, 84, 106

Sierra Club, 60, 79

"SLAPP suit," 63, 112, 145

"smart growth," 102

Sorenson, Mike, 10, 134–135

sprawl. *See* urban sprawl

State of the Lakeshore Basin Report. *See* Wisconsin Department of Natural Resources

Stewardship Program (Wisconsin Department of Natural Resources), 10, 26, 27, 48–49, 97, 110, 123, 124, 126, 129, 130–134, 136, 153, 157; Urban Green Space Program, 110, 130

Strategic Lawsuits Against Public Participation. *See* "SLAPP suit"

strategy in land battles, 16, 45–54

stress from land battles, managing, 18, 152–159

subdivisions, 24, 38, 87, 144

taxes: effects of development on, 6, 15, 22, 26, 49, 91, 92, 94, 95, 96, 141, 142, 143, 147, 149; laws, federal, 118; legal advice regarding, 59; records and deeds, 29; struc-

turing, in real estate transactions, 139. *See also* 501(c)(3) entity; land conservancy (or land trust)

television, 107. *See also* media

TeWinkle, William, 62–63, 64

Thompson, Tommy, 7

traffic congestion, 22, 49, 93, 97, 105, 147, 150

Trout Unlimited, 81

Trust for Public Lands, 119

universities, 15, 82, 110, 122, 128, 129. *See also individual universities*

University of Wisconsin, Green Bay, 39–40, 83–84, 128

University of Wisconsin, Madison, 27, 39, 82–83, 127

University of Wisconsin, Manitowoc, 83–84

University of Wisconsin, Milwaukee, 27

University of Wisconsin, Sheboygan, 83–84

University of Wisconsin Extension, 102

Urban Green Space Program. *See* Stewardship Program (Wisconsin Department of Natural Resources)

Urban Land Institute, 94–95, 99, 149

urban planning, 27, 82–83

Urban Planning Institute, 99

urban sprawl, 26, 27, 82–83, 95, 115, 126

variances, 9, 20, 21, 23, 24, 56, 86; in Point Creek land battle, 38, 39, 129, 153. *See also* zoning

village boards, 86, 87, 88. *See also* Cleveland Village Board

wastewater treatment, 6, 26, 29, 42, 46, 92, 93, 95, 96, 141. *See also* septic systems; sewage and water services

West Foundation, 10, 69, 106, 134–135, 153

wetlands, 4, 12, 20, 24, 128; coastal, of Manitowoc County, 39, 127

Wiesmueller, Bill, 124–125

wildlife, 1, 4, 9, 12, 40, 93, 94, 148, 150; management of, 26, 27. *See also* habitat

Wimpffen, Otto and Laurel, 13, 43–44, 53, 66–68, 70, 116

Wisconsin Coastal Management Program, 39, 90, 102, 122–127, 129–133, 153, 154

Wisconsin Conservation Corps, 90

Wisconsin Department of Administration, 27, 155

Wisconsin Department of Natural Resources (DNR), 159; designation of Class 1 trout stream by, 4; Land Legacy Study of, 39, 127; role of, in Fischer Creek land battle, 7, 27, 46, 81, 97–98, 108,

113, 155; role of, in Point Creek land battle, 11, 51–52, 63, 65, 69, 110, 122, 128; and the State of the Lakeshore Basin Report, 128; wetlands data compilation of, 127–128. *See also* Stewardship Program

Wisconsin Public Television, 107

Wisconsin State Legislature, 83, 111, 119, 154; Joint Finance Committee of, 70, 110, 130–133. *See also* lobbying

Woodland Dunes (Manitowoc County), 81

YMCA, 85

zoning, 5, 13, 14, 15–16, 20, 21, 25, 56, 57, 140, 143; changes, procedures required for, 23–24, 86; in Fischer Creek land battle, 155; in Hika Conservancy land battle, 43, 52–53, 65–68, 70, 91, 109, 138. *See also* variances